BUILDING SMART
TEAMS

To our husbands:
sources of motivation, inspiration,
perspiration, exasperation, and, most of all, devotion.

BUILDING SMART TEAMS

A Roadmap to High Performance

Carol A. Beatty
Queen's University

Brenda A. Barker Scott
Queen's University

SAGE Publications
Thousand Oaks ▪ London ▪ New Delhi

For information:

Sage Publications, Inc.
2455 Teller Road
Thousand Oaks, California 91320
E-mail: order@sagepub.com

Sage Publications Ltd.
1 Oliver's Yard
55 City Road
London EC1Y 1SP
United Kingdom

Sage Publications India Pvt. Ltd.
B-42, Panchsheel Enclave
Post Box 4109
New Delhi 110 017 India

Printed in the United States of America on acid-free paper.

Library of Congress Cataloging-in-Publication Data

Beatty, Carol Anne, 1943-
Building smart teams: roadmap to high performance/Carol A. Beatty and Brenda A. Barker Scott.
    p. cm.
Includes bibliographical references and index.
ISBN 0-7619-2956-8 (pbk.)
   1. Teams in the workplace. 2. Performance. I. Scott, Brenda A. Barker (Brenda Ann Barker), 1962- II. Title.
HD66.B43 2005
658.4′022—dc22

                                        2004003258

04   05   06   07   08   09   10   9   8   7   6   5   4   3   2   1

Acquiring Editor:	Al Bruckner
Editorial Assistant:	MaryAnn Vail
Production Editor:	Claudia Hoffman/Tracy Alpern
Copy Editor:	Eric Tucker, Publication Services, Inc.
Typesetter:	C&M Digitals (P) Ltd.
Indexer:	Sheila Bodell
Cover Designer:	Glenn Vogel

Contents

Acknowledgments

We first decided to write this book while working with a union management group that was intent on learning to collaborate more effectively to save their company. We will always be grateful to that wonderful group, especially a couple of creative individuals who came up with a cartoon that really put the whole team training week into perspective. It showed a mountain-climbing team, tied together and to each other, ascending a very steep cliff. It was an apt metaphor for what we were trying to achieve with that team—to train them to take a very uncertain and potentially perilous journey together, as a real team. Our heartfelt thanks go out to Al, Don, Geoff, Hardy, Rick, and Wayne, the original group at Peregrine Oshawa that sparked the idea behind this book.

Up until we met them, we had been designing and carrying out training to create high-performing teams for a number of years and had collected a number of excellent exercises and training aids, but we had never committed anything to paper.

We'd also like to thank all the other fine people we've worked with over the past five years, who have encouraged us to keep raising the bar on our training and who have contributed so much to deepening our understanding of high-performance teams. Our ideas have also evolved from working with other consultants and trainers, in particular Deborah Harrington-Mackin and Kathy Wills.

Special thanks also to Kirsteen MacLeod, who has provided expert suggestions and editing to improve the readability of our original manuscript. And thanks to the good people at Sage, including editor Al Bruckner, editorial assistant MaryAnn Vail, and production editor Tracy Alpern for having faith in us and in the usefulness of this book.

Finally, thanks to our husbands and families, who spent many a night alone as we researched, wrote, traveled, and trained, spreading our knowledge about how to create high-performance teams.

About This Guide

What makes for high-performance teams? To answer this question, we have been collecting comprehensive data on more than 80 academic and 185 industry teams since 1993. In all, we have surveyed more than 350 individuals in MBA learning teams and close to 1,500 members of work teams in both the public and private sectors.

In *Building Smart Teams*, we share our findings with you, providing the theory and tools you'll need to get fast, smart results from your work group.

In Chapter 1, we begin by synthesizing the latest thinking on why high-functioning teams are so important to organizational success. Then, we introduce our Team Effectiveness Model, a roadmap designed to guide teams on their journey to maximum group ingenuity. The good news is that all of the key success factors we have identified in the model are either skills that can be learned, or structures or processes that can be put in place.

Chapters 2, 3, and 4 each expand on one of the three key success factors of high-performing groups: team management practices, problem-solving skills, and conflict-handling skills.

In Chapter 5, we explore how to maintain a team-friendly climate that will encourage successful team collaboration within your organization.

The final section of the book provides structured, stimulating exercises that dovetail with the text, guiding you in your explorations as you create your own smart teams.

The purpose of the Team Effectiveness Model we've described in the guide is not to dictate the one best way for teams to behave. Rather, we hope to help team members build skills and implement processes that will increase the likelihood that they will excel. Within our model, there is ample room for teams to discover their own unique culture, performance strategies, and paths to success.

We hope you enjoy the journey!

Building Smart Teams: A Roadmap to High Performance   1

An Introduction

Smart Teams: The What For and Why

When teams comprise people with various intellectual foundations and approaches to work . . . ideas often combine and combust in exciting and useful ways.

Theresa Amabile (1999, p. 13)

Today, most organizations face the difficult challenge of regaining or maintaining a competitive advantage. With intense global competition and deregulation, no organization is exempt from the myriad forces creating the need for organizational renewal (see, for example, Beer & Nohria, 2000; Ghoshal & Bartlett, 2000). In fact, it has become somewhat cliché to talk about the extraordinary complexity we face in our work environments.

When we ask managers to identify the factors and trends driving the need for change in their organizations, they typically identify technological innovations, higher customer expectations, new global entrants, increased or decreased government regulations, and changing consumer demands and demographics as being at the top of their lists. While the implications of these forces play out differently in each organization, all organizations must become adept at reading and responding swiftly and proactively to the competitive forces. According to Goleman, Kaufmann, and Ray (1992), the ability to acquire, interpret, and act upon information with innovations in processes and products is a core competitive capability.

To do this, organizations require ingenuity—clever, imaginative, out-of-the-box responses that allow them to flex with their many competitive demands. This means that they must create favorable conditions for people to spontaneously come together to share knowledge and learn as they explore organizational challenges and identify novel ideas. Undoubtedly, teamwork is the most efficient way for organizations to encourage and harness this creative potential.

By teamwork, we mean real teamwork, whereby the right people with the right skills, knowledge, and perspectives join to collectively explore challenges, generate creative solutions, and work diligently to build the necessary support and commitment for implementation. Not surprisingly, teams have been identified as an integral ingredient in developing and sustaining a high-performance work culture. In his critical examination of people management practices, Jeffrey Pfeffer described what leads to organizational health. At the root of these people management practices is teamwork, "with decentralized decision-making and empowerment as the basic principle of organizational design" (Pfeffer, 1999, p. 64).

Apart from the many performance benefits, working in teams can also facilitate employee satisfaction; in fact, our research shows that team performance and satisfaction are highly related (Beatty, 1997). As employees continue to seek meaningful and developmental work opportunities, teams can provide a powerful avenue for learning, flexibility, job enhancement, and empowerment (Campion, Medsker, & Higgs, 1993). Real-time learning occurs as members expand their expertise, knowledge, and experience.

Despite its many advantages, working in teams is increasingly hard work in today's rapidly evolving business world. For the team's work to be relevant, their challenge is by nature complex. Why would an organization invest precious time and resources in an irrelevant challenge? The days of teamwork for the sake of teamwork are long over. Today's teams are charged with complex, high-stakes issues that require clever innovation, resourcefulness, and disciplined action.

On many occasions, we have asked teams to assess the complexity of their challenges. More often than not, they describe initiatives that require members to expand their thinking, to learn from each other and others outside of the immediate team, to build on existing know-how, to apply knowledge in new ways, and to go through many iterations of collecting and analyzing data before a solution emerges.

Apart from the obvious task complexity, teams also report that their challenges involve complex relationships; more and more their challenges require that they work with and involve many stakeholders, often with competing interests, biases, and ways of working. We refer to challenges with high task and relationship complexity as *jamais vu* challenges, in which team members have never been there or done that before together. *Déjà vu* challenges, on the other hand, are those with low complexity that the team has already mastered in the past.

Déjà vu challenges are relatively simple to deal with because teams have developed expertise over time to handle them, and members follow a prescribed process with set roles and responsibilities. But today, teams are more often confronted with challenges they have never encountered before and where there is no specific path to success. These *jamais vu* challenges are all around us: Constitutional reform, culture change, implementing a merger or acquisition, or new strategy formation are all examples of systemwide change initiatives that require team members to manage complex relationships while forging a new path.

So as the complexity of our business challenges increases, so

Today's Teams: The Move From *Déjà Vu* to *Jamais Vu*

Executive development expert Peter DeLisle's typology of task and relationship complexity, which we have adapted, is a useful tool for considering a team's work. A challenge with low task and relationship complexity is one in which familiar team members follow a prescribed process with defined procedures. We call these *déjà vu* challenges—in other words, challenges that the team has experienced before. Examples may include the admitting and treatment process followed by emergency room attendants, or protocols adopted by firefighters for attending to a blaze.

In contrast, a challenge with high task and relationship complexity is one where the players may not be familiar with working together and do not have explicit protocols or direct experience and know-how to apply to the task at hand. We call these *jamais vu* challenges, which involve issues that the team has never encountered before, while team members must learn to work together at the same time. No one person has the right answer or all of the relevant expertise, and the team must explore and experiment to discover a solution.

An example of a highly complex challenge was the severe acute respiratory syndrome (SARS) epidemic, which was first reported in Asia in February 2003 and quickly spread to more than two dozen countries within months. Dubbed the mystery illness, SARS eventually claimed 44 lives in Canada and 238 in Asia. In Canada, the absence of a national body for disease control meant that specialists and health care officials had to join forces quickly to first identify the mystery virus and then, through trial-and-error experimentation, develop protocols for diagnosis,

(continued)

(Continued)

treatment, prevention and disseminate critical information to those in the field. Their laudable efforts, although imperfect, led to the eventual containment of the highly infectious virus.

With *jamais vu* tasks, teams operating in the same old ways and using the same mindsets, processes, and tools designed for less complex challenges will find themselves in deep water. Messy and ambiguous challenges, ones that are hard to design and have no prescribed right answer, require members to explore, experiment, and evolve their thinking together. These challenges require team protocols designed to encourage both task ingenuity and relationship ingenuity. Simply put, these teams must be designed to tap into the know-how and perspectives of relevant stakeholders to create relevant, workable solutions that members and their partners are energized to implement.

does the need for real teamwork. Well-designed teams can provide the task and relationship ingenuity to survive and thrive in *jamais vu* territory. Yet real teamwork is often lacking. In the public sphere, for example, stories abound of government councils, tasked with greater responsibility, reduced budgets, and a more demanding public, spending their time bickering rather than finding ways to create better results. In organizations, real senior teams are largely a myth (Katzenbach, 1997), even though cohesive leadership from the top team is more important than ever to the process of creating a mission, a guiding vision, and a strategy. Throughout the organization, teams must plan, implement, and build support for the many change projects that are

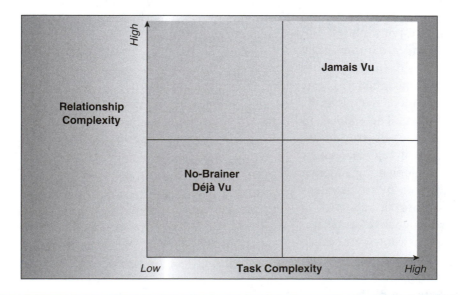

Figure 1.1   Our Team Challenges

happening all at once. Often, we see half-hearted attempts that fail as members give up prematurely in the face of apparent resistance.

Effective teamwork at all levels of the organization is now a necessity, the foundation for the flexible, empowered, and high-performance culture that organizations are desperately seeking to create. So the question is, how do managers and leaders go about organizing for real teamwork?

To provide a roadmap to guide team leaders on this journey, we have developed the Team Effectiveness Model based on comprehensive research. Our model identifies the critical processes and skills that leaders need to get their teams up and running quickly and to create smart teams that excel at accomplishing their objectives.

Your Roadmap: Introducing the Team Effectiveness Model

We've all been part of successful and unsuccessful teams, and as such, we all have firsthand experience of the benefits and frustrations of team membership. While some group experiences are very fulfilling, with members becoming highly skilled at working together, others are frustrating, with members developing interpersonal conflicts that are counterproductive to team progress.

These experiences have taught us that participating on a team is not necessarily easy, and for many of us it does not come naturally. Team success depends on a number of factors, including attracting the right people to work on a common goal, enabling them to begin working together well and quickly, setting and adhering to performance schedules, and, inevitably, handling the interpersonal stresses that occur when people work together closely.

Perhaps the greatest challenge for a team member is the struggle and resulting tension that arises from being an individual—with one's own talents, biases, values, beliefs, interests, and ways of working—versus being a member of a team. Being part of a team requires members to involve others in making important decisions, to share critical information openly, and, at times, to sacrifice one's personal agenda for the good of the team. The challenge, of course, is to harness the group creativity that comes from an open exchange of ideas and opinions to produce an integrated solution that builds on the best of the individual thinking. Maintaining the balance between fostering diverse thinking and controlling these differences is often easier said than done (Burke, 1988).

So despite the many potential benefits of effective teamwork, including increased performance, improved decision quality, high commitment to group decisions, and increased job satisfaction (Hackman, 1990), team membership requires a new orientation to working, and most members need to *learn* how to be part of a team. Marvin Weisbord (1987) suggests that management teams actually have to unlearn "bad habits" because most organizational cultures have rewarded individual results and competitive behaviors, not cooperation and teamwork.

We believe that most individuals can learn to be good team members and reap the personal and professional rewards of team membership. Our research suggests that by undertaking several key activities, organizations can give their teams a strong foundation for success.

SIGNPOSTS TO GROUP INGENUITY: CRITICAL PROCESS AND SKILLS

Our model (Beatty, 2003) has narrowed the key success factors of high-performing teams to three critical sets of processes and skills. These key processes and skills predict both team performance (how well the team performs its assigned tasks) and team satisfaction (the extent to which members enjoy and derive personal gains from their team experiences). They include the following:

❖ Team management practices

❖ Problem-solving skills

❖ Conflict-handling skills

We like to think of the building of these skills as base camp for teams; that is, the work involved in developing effective team management practices, problem-solving skills, and conflict-handling skills is akin to base camp for mountain climbers. Just as successful mountain climbers must spend sufficient time preparing for their ascent by planning their route, testing equipment, delineating roles and responsibilities, adapting to the climate, and stocking supplies, teams must devote sufficient time and energy to developing effective team management practices, problem-solving abilities, and conflict-handling processes. As teams spend time building these essential skills, they learn to work effectively together.

ALL FOR ONE: TOP TEAM MANAGEMENT PRACTICES

Team management practices refer to the overall level of team commitment, social functioning, and task approaches of the team. With effective team management practices in place, a group possesses the following characteristics:

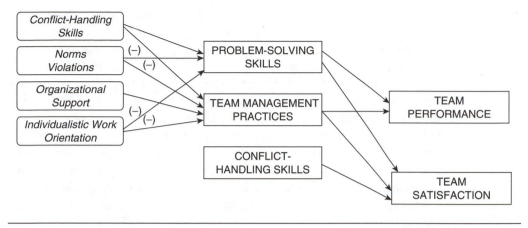

Figure 1.2   Team Effectiveness Model

Task Processes

1. A common purpose with set goals, priorities, and task strategies

2. Defined tasks with clear authority and responsibilities assigned to members

Social Processes

3. Protocols and norms for working together—that is, processes for problem solving, conflict handling, evaluation, inclusion, and so forth

4. Clear roles and responsibilities to ensure that members' talents are fully utilized

Commitment

5. Committed members who are willing to pull their share and exert extra effort to ensure that the team tasks are completed on schedule

Good team management practices are very important to establish in the early stages of team development. As such, we highly recommend that team-building efforts begin with the team defining their purpose and goals, followed by roles and responsibilities, and then norms and protocols. As the team develops and works together, commitment and motivation should naturally follow. Later on, the team management practices may become second nature to the high-performance team and may even go unnoticed and unappreciated. However, establishing these practices up front can ensure that the team gets off to a good start.

From Predicament to Ingenuity: Problem Solving for Pros

Teams with strong problem-solving skills possess the communication and interpersonal skills necessary to work effectively. Team members are *patient communicators*; they work hard to understand each other and make themselves understood. Difficulties in understanding are attributed to the communications process in general, not to other members' failings. Group members follow an agreed-upon process for exploring problems and challenges, collecting information, developing options, and evaluating and selecting a workable solution. It is the combination of these skill sets that fosters synergistic decision making, whereby the team together develops solutions that are better than the sum of individual ideas.

From Chaos to Creativity: Conflict Handling for Results

Conflict-handling skills refer to the group's ability to resolve conflicts as they occur. Teams that demonstrate good team management practices and possess problem-solving skills experience less conflict. However, conflict does occur and high-performance teams have a strategy in place to deal with it. They *do not* avoid thorny issues. They work to identify and understand the underlying issues and to deal with them effectively. In dealing with the difficult situation, members do not let issues fester and grow into interpersonal stresses between members. Rather, they address the issues and move on, putting in place a process or protocol for resolving similar conflicts in the future.

Measuring Your Team's Progress

How do you measure team success? When we ask teams this question, most identify task performance variables, such as accomplishing their goal or exceeding customer requirements, as well as personal satisfaction variables, such as feelings of accomplishment, mastery of new skills, and a sense of belonging. We suggest that both are critically important to team effectiveness.

Intuitively, this makes a lot of sense. If the team works cohesively but does not deliver the performance required by its customers or supervisors, it is not high functioning. Conversely, teams that achieve their goals but do not develop the goodwill and commitment of their members only frustrate their ability to work together on future tasks. It is when both task and social functioning are high that teams can excel by creating a climate where group members commit to participating fully and become personally invested in the team.

Therefore, our model provides a measure of both team performance and team satisfaction. Team performance measures the degree to which the group agrees that its productive output—whether a product, service, or decision—meets the needs for quality, quantity, and service expected by its customers. Team satisfaction measures the extent to which group members enjoy being a member of the team and experience the social rewards of membership, such as learning, development, and a sense of belonging. Satisfied team members are committed to achieving their tasks and remaining on the team.

We found that measuring performance and satisfaction was much more complex than simply counting outputs. First, we asked the team sponsors—professors for the learning teams or managers for the industry teams—to subjectively assess how well their teams were doing with respect to both progress toward goals and satisfaction among members. Rather surprisingly, we found that both professors and managers had very little intuitive sense of how well their teams were doing. In fact, many were very surprised to find that their teams were experiencing difficulties.

Next, we attempted to measure task-related outputs such as marks for the learning teams and product or service outputs for the industry teams. Here we also found low consistency between the manager's or professor's assessment of the team's performance and the team's assessment of how well they were doing. We also found a high variance of assessments among the different professors and managers to whom the teams reported. In other words, we found that various managers or professors did not agree about how well the team was performing. So we decided that the team's own assessment was probably the best one. Teams may well inflate their ratings of performance. But if all teams do so to roughly the same extent, it still allows us to array them on a measurement scale from lower to higher performance. In other words, we can compare them and analyze them statistically.

In the end, we chose to rely on each team's assessment of their performance and satisfaction levels. Only the team truly knows how well it is performing and how skilled members are at working together, given the many challenges and obstacles encountered en route to goal completion. In support of this approach, we found a high degree of consistency among the team members' scores for performance and satisfaction, adding credence to our view that the team members know best how they are doing.

How to Maintain High-Octane Group Functioning

At the heart of improving group effectiveness is the ability of group members to reflect on what they are doing well and how they need to improve—that is, what they need to start doing, what they should stop doing, and what they should continue doing. However, most groups find it difficult to examine their behavior on their own and wonder where to begin. Our model provides teams with a diagnostic guide for assessing how well they are doing and for determining where they need to focus their energy on skill development.

So, for example, teams often ask us questions like, "We got off to a great start, but it seems as though we are losing focus. How do we get it back?" or "Some members are coming late or not completing their team work on time. How do we rebuild their commitment to the team?" or "Some members can't work together; what should we do?"

Just as a physician uses patients' vital signs to determine their health and detect possible ailments, teams can use the Team Effectiveness Model to assess where and how the team needs to improve. When stalled, teams can do an overall diagnosis using our Team Effectiveness Model Gap Analyzer (see page 12, or page 115 in the Exercises section) to obtain an overview of areas of most and least effectiveness. Next, a team can zoom in directly on the three key success factors of high-functioning teams using our specific diagnostic instruments:

Team Management Practices: Do members understand and agree on their task? Have team members created and internalized their team norms of conduct? Do members have the necessary skills, expertise, perspectives, and resources to do their work? Is the team aligned with the interests of its stakeholders? Do team members feel supported by the organization? Do members feel safe to express their views and contribute fully? Are members committed to exerting the necessary effort for task accomplishment? (For a more detailed analysis, refer to the Team Management Practices Assessment on page 117 for an instrument to provide the answers to these questions.)

Problem Solving: Are members patient communicators? Do they take the time to truly understand each other's points of view and contributions? Do members evaluate potential ideas and solutions before they discard them or adopt them? Do they build on each other's ideas to create synergistic solutions? Are simple decisions overanalyzed? Are members following an agreed-upon problem-solving process for collecting information, exploring options, evaluating solutions, and making decisions, or are they jumping to conclusions? (Refer to the Team Problem-Solving Assessment on page 145 for a way to explore these issues with your team.)

Conflict Handling: Are members avoiding conflict? Do members examine all views or simply avoid conflict to speed decision making along? Are important decisions being made prematurely? Do thorny issues remain under the table? Are disruptive behaviors blocking the team from achieving their goals? (Refer to the Handling Problems in Team Discussion Assessment on page 182 to help answer these questions.)

Each of the three chapters that follow is devoted to one of these key factors for effective teams: team management practices, problem solving, and conflict handling. In addition, we've included structured and stimulating exercises to guide you along the path toward creating your own high-efficiency teams.

The Team Effectiveness Gap Analyzer provides an excellent place for a team to begin, allowing an overall assessment both of what is in good shape and of where there are gaps that need to be bridged. Teams can learn whether they are ready, getting ready, moving slowly, or stalled in each of the three key areas for working together effectively.

Team Effectiveness Model Gap Analyzer

Level	Team Management Practices	Problem Solving	Conflict Handling
4 Ready ("Watch our dust!")	Team purpose and goals are clearly defined and compelling and our whole team is focused on achieving them. Members are working collectively, tapping the full potential of all and creating superior results. We have a well-defined approach for tackling our challenges and it is working for us. Relationships with key stakeholders are well defined, productive, and focused on the overall goals. Our team norms are well established and everybody abides by them. All individuals are included and respected as full, contributing members. All members are fully committed to the team and its purpose.	Our team creates ingenious "1 + 1 > 2" solutions. We use communication patience skills to foster dialogue, share important knowledge, and explore assumptions. We use synergy tools to help members expand their thinking, generate and build on ideas, and evaluate those ideas to arrive at superior solutions. We use the right process tools to guide our work. We discuss and agree upon sound approaches to problem solving, and we collect the relevant information before jumping into discussions about solutions.	We have established a team climate that welcomes and accepts diverse points of view, and our members feel safe to express themselves fully. We understand that conflict is a normal and natural part of team life. When conflicts do occur, we pause and discuss how we can move forward. We then develop a protocol to help us prevent similar conflicts in the future. We do not allow conflict to become personalized.
3 Getting Ready ("We're on the right track")	Team purpose and goals are becoming clear. The team is on the right track for completing our purpose, vision, priorities, and goals. Members are committed to working collectively, and we are learning how to tap into the full potential of all. We are defining/tweaking our approach for tackling our challenges, and more often than not, the approach is working for us. Results are coming nicely. Relationships with key stakeholders are well defined and for the most part are working. We are establishing team norms. Most of the time we are unafraid to confront difficulties and to discuss ways of working together more productively. Commitment to the team is fairly high.	Our team is learning how to create breakthrough "1 + 1 > 2" solutions. When we use communication patience and synergy tools, we arrive at superior solutions. Our process tools are helping guide our work and expand our creative thinking. We are beginning to be disciplined about how we approach problem solving and have put more structure around our discussions.	We're working hard to promote a team climate that welcomes diverse views so that members feel safe to express themselves. When conflicts do occur, we pause and discuss how we can move forward.

Level	Team Management Practices	Problem Solving	Conflict Handling
2 Moving Slowly ("We're not on track yet")	Loosely defined goals provide some focus and direction. We're beginning to recognize that a clear purpose and vision are important. We recognize that we are not tapping the full potential of all, and as a result, we're not producing the results expected of us. We do not have the right approach or strategy for tackling our challenges, and this is slowing us down. Experience has taught us that we need to foster relationships with key stakeholders. We're beginning to identify, clarify, and develop relationships with key groups. Team norms are loosely defined. Sometimes we do not live up to the great ideas that we had initially discussed for working together. Commitment of some members to the team is uneven.	Our team creates "1 + 1 = 2" solutions. Our team meetings are focused on sharing information from each member's area of responsibility. We do not use processes and techniques to identify common challenges, share relevant information, build on each other's ideas, or generate solutions that benefit all members and stakeholders. At best, we operate as a group instead of a real team. We are not disciplined in our problem-solving approach, and our discussions seem at times to be going in circles. We do not base our discussions nearly enough on sound information, but rather on members' opinions and intuitions.	Our team climate does not always welcome diverse views, and members are often uncomfortable with expressing their thoughts and feelings. We have no protocols in place to help us manage conflict effectively. As a result, conflicts often steer us off track and block us from moving forward.
1 Stalled ("We are spinning our wheels")	We have no concept of our purpose or vision. We do not have a useful approach or strategy for tackling our challenges, and this is slowing us down. Roles and responsibilities are unclear, resulting in confusion and frustration. Relationships with key stakeholder groups are unclear or not viewed as important. Team norms do not exist. People disagree over how we should be working together, and conflict is glossed over or ignored. Some members are not committed to the team at all.	Our team creates "1 + 1 < 2" solutions. Our team meetings are chaotic, with members interrupting, grandstanding, withholding information, and so on. Our inability to generate workable solutions stops progressive action and blocks people from moving forward on important issues.	Our team climate does not welcome diverse views and members do not feel safe to express themselves. We have no protocols in place to help us manage conflict effectively. As a result, conflicts often steer us off track and block us from moving forward. Members have personalized the conflicts, and cliques have formed to create "we–they" separations.

Creating Smart Team Management Practices 2

Team Management Practices: Signpost #1 for Team Success

Team management practices—one of the three key factors identified in the Team Effectiveness Model—are the most important determinant of a team's level of competency.

Teams with strong team management practices share key capabilities, which fall under three main headings: **task processes**, which help focus members on the task at hand; **social processes**, which help define what appropriate team behavior is and help maintain good relationships, both internally and externally; and **team commitment processes**, which ensure that members are energized for collective work. Useful task and social practices build commitment.

Extensive literature supports this, yet in our experience, organizations are not applying this well-documented knowledge. We often begin our team-building workshops by asking participants to answer yes or no to a series of questions adapted from William Dyer (1994) as follows:

- ❖ How many of you believe that teamwork is essential for achieving results in your organizations?

- ❖ How many of your organizations espouse teamwork as a core value?

- ❖ How many of you regard team management as a leadership core competence?

- ❖ How many of you spend time developing the team(s) that you lead?

- ❖ How many of your bosses are doing anything to develop their teams?

- ❖ How many of your top management teams spend time developing their teamwork?

- ❖ How many of you believe that your senior leadership is committed to effective teamwork in your organization?

Research Note

Extensive literature supports our view of what creates high-performance teams. For example, Hackman (2002) identified internal work motivation, core norms of conduct, team composition, and compelling direction as key team design elements for high team performance. Beckhard (1972) identified four criteria for team building, including set goals, work allocation according to roles and responsibilities, procedures and processes, and relationships. Similarly, Sundstrom (1999) identified the importance of clear purpose, scope, authority, resources, accountability, reporting relationships, and appropriate staffing.

Time and again we find that while the great majority of people emphatically state that teamwork is a core value, few participants report that they or their bosses are doing anything to develop teamwork in their organizations.

Why the gap between knowing and doing? Our participants offer four key reasons. First, managers seem to believe that teamwork happens spontaneously. Their assumption appears to be that teams will just naturally organize themselves to tap the full potential of all members. Next, they report that teamwork is not overtly recognized and rewarded within their organizations. While teamwork may be an espoused value, the rewards go to individuals and not team contributors. Third, our participants suggest that bad team experiences have soured their enthusiasm for teamwork. Jon Katzenbach (1997) uses the term *pseudo-teams* to refer to the nonproductive phenomenon of teams created solely for the sake of having teams. Groups that are more focused on togetherness than on performance have made *team* a four-letter word. And finally, our participants suggest that team leaders simply don't know how to design and support teams for success. With a plethora of advice in the marketplace on what constitutes high-performing teams—much of it confusing and anecdotal—team leaders simply don't know what to do. As a result, precious time and energy gets wasted on efforts that lead nowhere.

And so, contrary to the hopes and high expectations of many team implementers, most teams do not become high-performing ones. Whether the team is formed to prevent a looming crisis, to create innovations in service delivery, or to develop a new product, simply assigning members to a team does not make a team.

More on the Model—Task, Social, and Commitment Strategies: A Roadmap to Effective Teams

If real teams are required to do important and relevant work, then how do we design for real teamwork? Our research and practice indicate that real teams can in fact be built and that the development of team management practices, in stages and over time, is the most critical determinant of team success. Our approach to designing sound team management practices integrates three critical concepts: task strategies, social strategies, and commitment strategies, which together provide the foundation for real teamwork (see Figure 2.1).

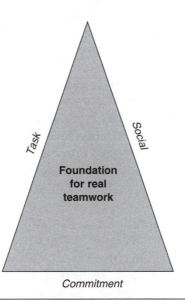

Figure 2.1   Foundation for Real Teamwork

Task strategies—The goals, activities, work processes, tools, and technology the members use to achieve their overall purpose

Social strategies—Processes and protocols to satisfy people's needs for voice, meaningful involvement, and relationships

Commitment strategies—The understanding that real commitment to the team, whereby members are energized to make the team's goals happen, develops from both a meaningful, relevant task (task strategies) and an enabling, respectful environment (social strategies)

The more complex and ambiguous the team's challenge, the more important both the task and social strategies become. Teams are often confronted with challenges that are not easily defined and that have no specific path to success. (See page 3 for a detailed description of *jamais vu* challenges.) With messy challenges, members must invest a significant effort in developing (a) a joint understanding of *why* they were called together (i.e., their ultimate purpose); (b) *what* they are expected to create together (i.e., their joint vision and strategy); and (c) *how* they will work together to ensure real voice, involvement, and transparency of decision making (members need to adopt roles, norms, and processes for working together to ensure the necessary collaboration).

Although developing task and social strategies ensures that members stay focused and committed to working collectively on their challenge, the unfortunate reality is that team building takes time—time that team members complain they do not have. Teams are often formed because a crisis is looming and their organizations demand results right away. Add in the fact that most members are assigned to teams in addition to their regular work responsibilities, and spending precious time on creating group norms or defining roles seems wasteful.

However, our research and practice have convinced us that the time spent creating team management practices is well worth the investment. Our grandmothers got it right when they said that an ounce of prevention is worth a pound of cure. Imagine how absurd it would be for a mountaineering group to begin ascending a mountain with no preparation or planning. Visualize the chaos, anger, frustration, and finger-pointing as group members realize that they do not have enough food, tents, or rope. Mountaineering teams know that preparation is essential for survival. Not only do they need to chart their course carefully, they also need to agree on protocols for working together in various scenarios. In this case, members' willingness and ability to adopt critical roles and responsibilities ultimately means the difference between life and death.

Similarly, when teams do not take the time to co-create their task, social, and commitment strategies, they expose themselves to the risk of failure. Without good team management practices, we see two general scenarios: Either the team tends to emphasize task strategies at the expense of social strategies, or vice versa. Either way, commitment to the team goals and to each other ultimately suffers. Some teams quite naturally favor the development of their social strategies. They create a participative climate, generate high involvement, and foster inclusiveness. While members may have a splendid time enjoying each other's company, the task becomes secondary. The result? Friendships may form, but relevant goals do not get set, ideas do not get tested, solutions do not get generated, and actions do not get planned. In short, the group is all talk and no action.

On the other hand, some groups naturally favor quick and decisive action. They meet, they plan, they do. In their haste to plan and strategize—with military precision, we might add—the art of exploration, involvement, and discovery is lost. The frequent result? Great plans focused on the wrong solution. Great plans, with no buy in from key stakeholder groups. Great plans that fall apart, because as support for the team's solution dwindles, members begin to blame each other for adopting a solution that they personally did not believe in. And so, we have much activity, but no real action.

The Team Management Practices Planner: Critical Conversations for Teams

The Team Management Practices Planner is designed to lead team members through a set of critical conversations to help them jointly create the following important strategies:

Task strategies—A compelling purpose, a meaningful challenge, the most appropriate strategy, processes and tools for working on the challenge, and authority and reporting relationships for doing the work

Social strategies—Membership, norms, and processes for group inclusion and collaboration

Commitment strategies—Personal, group, and professional benefits for the time, energy, and effort invested

As no two teams are alike, there is no single formula for the way a team works through the Team Management Practices Planner (see Figure 2.2). For new teams—or any teams that have not yet completed the exercise—we highly recommend discussion of all planner elements, but we do not prescribe a rigid format for how to cover them or for what they turn out to be. Existing teams will have different needs as they reassess and recalibrate team management practices in an ongoing process. For all teams, the value comes from the process of members sharing their expectations for team membership and coming to group agreements, which they can work through with the questions and exercises we've prepared. (See the exercises for effective team management practices beginning on page 117.)

		Element	Description	Tools/Exercises
1	*Task*	1. Purpose (p. 22)	The team's overall purpose or reason for being; it defines the group's overall challenge and provides clarity around focus.	*Marvin's Trends Mind Map* identifies factors impacting the team challenge and high-leverage priorities for action. *Defining Our Team Purpose* is a discussion tool to synthesize data from the mind map into a definitive team challenge.
		2. Vision and strategy (p. 24)	Begin with the end in mind by asking, "What will success look like?" Next, assess the gap between the ideal and current reality to identify priorities and strategies for taking action.	*Developing Team Vision and Strategy* identifies high-level objectives and the appropriate strategy to match the challenge.
		3. Goals and accountabilities (p. 30)	Allocating specific actions and expected results for each team member helps create goal accountability.	*Developing Clear, Motivating Goals and Accountabilities* details who will do what to accomplish the team's goals, as well as who needs to be consulted, informed, and involved.
		4. Authority and reporting structure (p. 33)	Negotiating your team's authority with the team sponsor provides clarity around project scope and boundaries.	*Negotiating Authority With Your Team Sponsor* helps you discuss the appropriate level of decision-making authority with your team sponsor as well as project scope.
2	*Social*	5. Team membership and contribution (p. 36)	The right membership is critical to team success. Members benefit from understanding why they and others have been selected and what unique contributions they are expected to make.	*Defining Team Membership and Contribution* provides discussion tools for identifying critical membership capabilities as well as identifying specific member responsibilities. See also *Resources Each Member Contributes to the Team*.
		6. Norms and protocols for working collectively (p. 38)	Team norms define "how we do things around here" and provide essential guidance for expected work habits and behaviors.	*Creating Helpful Norms and Protocols* promotes honest discussion about the strategies, behaviors, and attitudes that support or block success. The *Team Culture Audit* helps your team examine norms in depth.
		7. Roles (p. 41)	By assigning team roles for facilitation and process management, teams stay focused and on task.	Helpful team roles include the following: Process Facilitator Scribe Leader Timekeeper Coach
		8. Relationships and communications (p. 45)	Most teams must work with others to achieve their objectives. Forging these important relationships early on ensures that workable solutions get implemented.	The *Stakeholder Mapping* tool helps teams define key stakeholder needs and the appropriate involvement and/or communication strategy.
3	*Commitment*	9. Results and reflection (p. 48)	Assessing team functioning on a regular basis leads to team learning and improvement. When teams grow and adapt, members remain committed.	The *Team Effectiveness Gap Analyzer*, *Team Management Practices Assessment*, *Team Problem-Solving Assessment*, and *Team Conflict-Handling Assessment* all allow existing teams to monitor their progress.

Figure 2.2   Team Management Practices Planner

TASK PROCESSES: THE WHY, WHAT, AND HOW OF THE TEAM CHALLENGE

Task processes comprise the following actions and elements (see Figure 2.2):

❖ Members create a meaningful and well-defined purpose.

❖ Members develop specific goals and task strategies for achieving those goals.

❖ Members clarify their authority and reporting relationships with respect to their goals.

Element 1: **Purpose.** What is our raison d'être or core challenge?

Element 2: **Vision and strategy.** When we have completed our work, what will we have achieved? How did we do it? What processes and tools did we employ to guide our activities?

Element 3: **Goals and accountabilities.** What are our goals, activities, and expected results? How will we achieve these goals? Who is responsible for completing each task? How and when will we be measured?

Element 4: **Authority and reporting structure.** How much authority do we have? Who do we report to?

SOCIAL PROCESSES: FOSTERING INTERNAL AND EXTERNAL RELATIONSHIPS FOR COLLECTIVE WORK

Social processes comprise the following actions and elements (see Figure 2.2):

❖ Members have developed and abide by respectful norms of conduct for meetings and group work.

❖ Members clarify roles and allocate the way the work is performed according to team members' responsibilities and talents.

❖ Members foster effective working relationships with their stakeholders.

Element 5: **Team membership and contribution.** Do we have the best mix and number of members? Do our members have the requisite skills, knowledge, experience, and authority to successfully accomplish our purpose and goals? Are members assigned tasks and responsibilities to ensure that their talents are fully recognized? Are external resources used to supplement the expertise we have on our team?

Element 6: **Norms and protocols for working collectively.** What's expected of me? How should I participate? How do we do things around here? How will we approach problem solving and decision making? How will we handle disruptive behaviors and interpersonal conflicts? How and when will we review team functioning?

Element 7: **Roles.** Are roles and responsibilities clearly defined? Are leadership roles shared? Are members given the opportunity to learn and develop by assuming new roles and responsibilities?

Element 8: **Relationships and communications.** What relationships are we expected to develop with others outside of the team? How will we align our team purpose and tasks with the goals of other important stakeholders? How will we communicate with and involve our stakeholders?

COMMITMENT PROCESSES: FOSTERING AN ENERGIZED COMMITMENT BASE FOR COLLECTIVE WORK

Commitment processes comprise the following actions and elements (see Figure 2.2):

- ❖ All members feel that they are a real part of the team.
- ❖ Each member assumes responsibility for getting the work done.
- ❖ Members demand that everyone contribute to team tasks, especially over the long term.
- ❖ Members do not reveal confidential information to outsiders.
- ❖ Cliques do not form within the group.

Element 9: **Results and reflection.** From time to time, it is necessary for teams to stop and reflect on their progress and working relationships. Are we energized and focused or spinning our wheels? How are our stakeholder relationships helping us or impeding us? Is our process helping to foster the right kind of ingenuity? Are all members participating, involved, and taking responsibility for team results?

Creating Smart Team Practices: Using the Nine Planner Elements

TASK PROCESSES: THE WHY, WHAT, AND HOW

Planner Element #1: Articulating Your Purpose

The Big Question: Why are we here?
Creation of the team's *purpose* for being is an important first step for newly forming teams. Powerful team building occurs as members jointly

explore their challenge or opportunity to develop a deep appreciation of their raison d'être. Together, members can create a purpose that they all want to contribute to, one that is fulfilling and meaningful for each member (Weisbord, 1987).

While alignment around the team's purpose is critical for cohesive action, we often find that teams underinvest in building this essential understanding. It's virtually impossible for seven team members with seven versions of their core purpose and priorities to be productive. Eventually, this lack of alignment surfaces as pesky irritants such as conflict with respect to goals and priorities ("Why are we talking about business X? I thought we were here to discuss business Y"), turf battles ("Our department has always done it this way, so why change?"), and interpersonal squabbles.

A good team purpose has two key ingredients. First, it clarifies how the team's work will support the organization as a whole. This gives the team organizational relevance. Understanding how their challenge is critical to the organization's success is important because people want to work on issues that are linked to the success and viability of their organizations.

> **Team Purpose**
>
> What is your core challenge?
>
> **A good team purpose . . .**
>
> Creates organizational relevance
> Creates personal relevance

Second, the purpose should tap into *why* the team is important and relevant for each member. Most people are so overloaded that they simply will not invest time and energy in tasks that do not have meaning for them personally and professionally. In creating their purpose, members have the opportunity to think about and share why membership on the team is important to them and what they truly hope to achieve with each other. So whether the purpose is to improve product quality or to strengthen union–management relationships or to implement teamwork throughout the organization, team members are more likely to develop the will to invest in the work if it is meaningful and relevant.

To create a team purpose, we often ask members to participate in a series of exercises designed to tap into their commitment base. These exercises help members share their thoughts on the top priorities for team results from which they will identify short- and long-term goals for action. To assist with this discussion, we almost always begin by asking members to complete Marvin Weisbord's (Weisbord & Janoff, 1995) Trends Mind Map exercise to create a whole-systems perspective of the major factors creating the need for change (see Figure 2.3). This exercise helps the team brainstorm the many trends and events that are creating the team problem or challenge. From the ideas generated, members identify the driving forces behind their team's purpose as well as the important relationships and interconnections with other groups and processes.

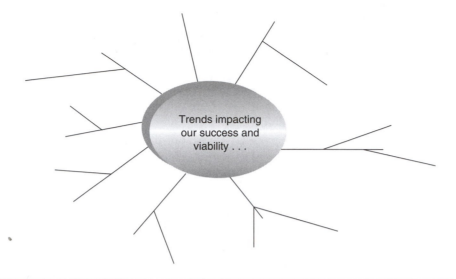

Figure 2.3   Marvin's Trends Mind Map

TEAM FITNESS EXERCISES

Select from Marvin's Trends Mind Map (see Figure 2.3) and Defining Our Team Purpose on page 121, or adapt them to create your own exercises.

Planner Element #2: Creating Your Team's Vision & Strategy—The Ideal "What"

Vision & Strategy

Begin with the end in mind.
Develop priorities for action.
Define approach for achieving priorities.

The Big Question: Where are we going?

When a team understands why it was formed, it can turn its attention to the important task of creating the ideal scenario: a vivid, detailed account of what life will be like, in business terms, after the mission has been achieved. We call this important step "beginning with the end in mind."

Part A: Visioning

Visioning has several steps, all of which must be completed for the exercise to have value and credibility.

1. The first is to ask members to design an ideal solution to their challenge. What would the solution look like right now (today) if they could have whatever they wanted?

2. The second involves reviewing this ideal solution for reality. Is it feasible—that is, do we have the know-how, technology, and people to make this work? Is it viable—that is, will it work here, given our operating environment and culture?

3. The third is to develop and organize priorities for action.

4. The fourth is to create supportive thinking for the changes.

Visioning Step 1: Begin With the End in Mind

Developing a vision requires imagination. It requires the team to think outside of their current reality so that they can dream of their ideal solution, unencumbered by present constraints. Some team members will naturally enjoy visioning, thinking of the possibilities and imagining their ideal solution with great gusto. Others will find the exercise difficult, as they are naturally rooted in the present and find it difficult to dream unencumbered by the present. In fact, we often find that team members and whole teams find it difficult to imagine what they *wish to create* because they are so focused on the constraints of their present reality.

It may be that North Americans are socialized to spot problems and not to generate creative, out-of-the-box solutions. After reviewing tape recordings of the messages that children receive from adults over a typical day, Professor John Adams found that more than 90% of the messages given by parents, teachers, and other authorities were about things the children should not do, could not do, or had done incorrectly (Reddy, 1994). Adams reasoned that these messages have shaped us to believe that there is one *right way* of doing things—and it is the way we do things now. We do not naturally think about how we want things to be, "mak[ing] it up the way we want it," but rather how to "make the best of what we already have."

Therefore, if we want our teams to think and operate from a right-brain, innovative mindset to create things the way *they want them to be*, we must explicitly help members to do so by building a bridge from the present to their ideal scenarios. Ways to do this appear on the next page.

Ways to Charge Up the Team's Creative Visioning

Try one of the scenarios below to help members think about what they truly want to create together.

❖ Imagine that your team is on the cover of *Fortune* as a model success story. What does the article say about your great success?
❖ Imagine that you have been away from your team on a special assignment for 3–5 years. As you rejoin the team on a catch-up meeting, what accomplishments will they tell you about?
❖ Write a letter to your organization's founder about your team's success. What accomplishments will you tell him/her about?
❖ Imagine that you are flying in a helicopter over your organization's building(s) and that you can see through the roofs into the many offices, hallways, and rooms (you have special goggles on). What do you see?

Key Visioning Questions

When thinking through the larger question of what the team will be doing differently once it has achieved its mission, consider the following:

Our Purpose

❖ What will our purpose be?
❖ What work will the team be doing?

Our Capabilities

❖ What projects will we be working on?
❖ What new skills and competencies will we have acquired?

Stakeholder Relationships

❖ What relationships will the team have fostered?
❖ Who will our customers be?
❖ Who will our suppliers be?
❖ Will we have partnerships? What will they look like?

Goals and Results

❖ What goals will we have achieved? How has achieving the goals assisted the organization?
❖ What other goals are we striving to achieve?
❖ How have we been rewarded?

Team Environment

❖ How are members relating to each other?
❖ What roles are we playing?
❖ What are we learning about?

Visioning Step 2: Assessing the Vision for Reality

The second step involves what Marvin Weisbord and Sandra Janoff (1995) refer to as the reality dialogue—assessing the vision for reality. During this phase, members have the opportunity to talk about what aspects of their ideal future they agree on and what aspects make sense from a business perspective. We suggest the following requirements for this important conversation: Is it feasible? (Do we have the know-how, technology, and people to make this work?) Is it viable? (Will it work here, given our operating environment and culture?)

From this discussion, members will have developed a list of real priorities that they can commit to working toward. It is at this phase of the process that members feel most comfortable, as they can use their logical thinking skills to decide what aspects of the vision they can reasonably achieve.

Visioning Step 3: Organizing Priorities

We recommend that members organize their priorities into several groupings, such as short-, medium-, and long-term or phase one, two, and three. This way, members will see how both their shorter- and longer-term priorities contribute to the realization of their ideal future. In addition, members will not feel compelled to tackle all the priorities simultaneously. In a recent survey of successful HR change initiatives, our colleague David Weiss (presentation at Queen's Industrial Relations Centre Strategic Human Resources Management Seminar, June 19, 2000) found that successful organizations tackled only one or two priorities at one time. This makes a lot of sense, as people cannot pursue everything that is important all at once. It serves the team well to focus their energy, as having too many priorities amounts to having no priorities at all.

Visioning Step 4: Supportive Thinking for Implementing Change

The final and often overlooked phase of visioning requires members to identify the present thinking and behaviors that will block them from achieving their priorities. For example, a manufacturing facility may create a priority to improve product quality. However, their present behavior pattern may be to get the product out the door and meet the numbers at all costs. This mismatch between the vision for quality and the present behavior for "numbers" must be acknowledged and discussed before meaningful change can occur.

Members also need to discuss what patterns of thinking and behavior they must create for the vision to become reality. What new habits do we need to create? What assumptions should we hold for customer service, quality, or innovation? How will we know we are on track? What behaviors do we need to reinforce, and what processes and systems will we put in place to reward them?

A Last Word on Vision: Expect It to Evolve

We believe that the team should hold the vision lightly, not tightly. For a vision to be useful, it must grow and change as the world around us changes. Constant input from stakeholders, sponsors, and customers will provide important food for thought on the next stages of the vision and on what elements should be a priority. As team members progress through achieving each stage of the vision, we suggest they review the next phases for relevance and meaning before tackling longer-term priorities.

Our group at Queen's University in Kingston, Ontario, recently did just that. In a session led by a colleague, we reviewed our vision of two years ago by listing on flipcharts the elements of the vision we "had completed," "were in the process of doing," and "had yet to do." This exercise worked beautifully, as we had the opportunity to celebrate all the activities we had completed, assess how our present activities were contributing toward achieving our vision, and assess whether we were still committed to activities set for our future. Interestingly enough, we dropped several priorities and added a few new ones. The exercise left us refreshed and committed to tackle our next challenges.

TEAM FITNESS EXERCISE

Refer to Developing Team Vision and Strategy on page 124.

Part B: Strategy—The Team's Overall Approach to Realizing the Vision

The Big Question: Given our purpose, vision, and priorities, what tools, techniques, and technologies do we need to apply?

We've all heard the adage "when the only tool you have is a hammer, every problem looks like a nail." And so it goes with teams. Just as specialists need to be equipped with the latest technology and thinking of their disciplines, teams need to be adept at identifying the processes, technologies, and tools that will facilitate the work they need to do.

The risk, of course, is that tools and processes incorrectly applied to the team's challenge will inadvertently send it down the wrong path, limiting the data collection, analysis, and exploration necessary to produce the right kind of group results. To optimize results and foster ingenuity, teams must match their approach to the challenge at hand, as different strategies apply to different types of challenges.

While there is no one path to success, a good approach, rooted in appropriate tools and technologies, will help get the intended results.

Teams that are focused on improving product quality will necessarily apply quality problem-solving tools such as "kaizen" or "Six Sigma." Teams that are focused on implementing change must become knowledgeable about change-management techniques. Teams creating new products or services will naturally apply creativity process and tools in their work. Thus, the discipline involved in knowing what tools to select and what expertise to acquire is a critical attribute of high-performing teams.

Although it is beyond the purview of this guide to review the exhaustive list of processes and tools associated with various team challenges, we do provide a series of key questions that will help your teams begin the process of discovering their core strategy for managing task and social processes.

Dannemiller Tyson Associates (2000) refer to this process of aligning people for collective work as creating *one heart, one brain*. This means that the whole team must become smart about *why* the initiative is necessary, *what* the initiative is intended to achieve, and *how* the initiative will be achieved (i.e., the best route for tackling the challenge). When all team members are involved in exploring and discovering the answers to these big questions, important learning occurs. As the team becomes smarter, its solutions also become smarter. The ideal approach to the team's challenge therefore involves a careful blending of the task strategies (the why, what, and how of the work) with the social strategies (the process that members will embark upon to learn and discover as they tackle the task).

Task Strategies

With respect to our purpose, vision, and priorities, what type of task ingenuity is required? Are we tasked with *innovation* in which we must create new knowledge, or are we tasked with *continuous improvement* to build on existing know-how?

If *innovation/creation* (or *jamais vu* challenges; see page 3 in Chapter 1 for details), we must ask the following questions:

- ❖ Are we required to create something totally new, or something that is just new for us?
- ❖ Who else has tackled a challenge like this one before?
- ❖ What do we need to learn from them?
- ❖ What critical know-how, expertise, best practices, and process tools exist to guide our work? How will we tap these resources?

If *continuous improvement*, we must ask ourselves the following:

- ❖ Are we required to improve a product, process, or system?

❖ If so, what is the best way to build on the existing knowledge base?

❖ What critical know-how, expertise, and best practices exist to guide us forward? How will we tap them?

❖ What are the standards that we must adhere to? What tools and techniques will help us meet these standards?

Social Strategies

❖ With respect to our team challenge, what type of social ingenuity is required?

❖ What is the best mix of people to achieve the required expertise and creativity?

❖ What processes will help us share and combine our know-how?

❖ What relationships do we need to build with others who have relevant knowledge and perspectives that we do not have?

❖ Who are the key people and groups that have a stake in this initiative? What do we need to know from them? What do they need to know from us?

❖ What level of consultation and involvement is required to develop a sufficient commitment base? What processes, tools, and technologies exist to facilitate this critical involvement?

❖ Will our process be iterative? Do we need to understand *A* before we can decide about *B*? Will we collect feedback and modify until we get it right? Is a test, pilot, or prototype required? Some examples of iterative approaches include the following:
  • Collect data—Discuss—Analyze—Decide
  • Collect data—Discuss—Seek input—Analyze—Decide
  • Collect data—Discuss—Seek input—Analyze—Refine—Seek input—Decide

The answers to these important questions will help your team develop a strategy for collecting, analyzing, and evaluating key information to make smart, sound discoveries.

Planner Element #3: Developing Clear Goals and Accountabilities

The Big Question: What are our goals and accountabilities?

<u>Part A: Developing Clear Goals—The "How" of Achieving Success</u>

Effective teams translate their purpose and priorities into clear goals, aligning members around practical tasks and results that they can monitor and measure. If the purpose is the proposed "why," and the vision the ideal "what" or destination, then the strategies and goals are the "how," that is, the specific roadmap the team will use to achieve success. Specific goals, such as increasing the client base by 25% or reducing cycle time by 10%, become a crucial way for members to assign the work, track effectiveness, and hold each other accountable.

The importance of clear goals for teams has been well documented in the research literature. Clear goals lead to higher performance and employee commitment when employees are involved in the goal-setting process (Steers & Porter, 1983). Moreover, receiving feedback on goal performance enhances productivity. For example, in one study, the researchers found that groups who received feedback solved their problems more accurately and were further motivated to solve new problems (Dessler, 1980). Moreover, clear goals with expected results and timelines provide focus, direction, pacing, and pressure (Katzenbach, 1997).

Simply put, goal setting works because it clarifies what is expected of the team, as well as how each member can contribute to goal achievement. A useful goal statement will state not only the end result to be achieved but also the strategy or process the team will use to achieve the goals. As the team specifies its overall goals and methods for achieving them—including the process, interim tasks, measurables and expected timelines, and who will be responsible for the work—it defines how members will hold each other accountable.

Research shows that timelines are important. When deadlines are absent, fuzzy, or constantly changing, groups invariably lose focus. Clear goals with expected results and timelines provide critical guidance around priorities and pace. Without the pres-

> ### How do you define your team's goals?
>
> Answer the questions below to find out:
>
> ❖ What are the specific objectives to be achieved?
>
> ❖ What key activities are required?
>
> ❖ What specific results or deliverables are expected of us? By whom?
>
> ❖ What are the expected dates for completion?
>
> ❖ How, when, and by whom will we be measured?
>
> ❖ At what milestones should we report results, and how should the results be reported?

sure of timelines, it is hard to keep the momentum, as the "busy work" of the team's day-to-day activities tends to get in the way (Hackman, 1990).

Part B: Accountability Charting

One of the most important conversations for team members is the discussion around accountabilities. While the team, as a whole, is accountable for achieving its overall purpose and goals, each team must go through the important process of identifying who can best carry out each of the subgoals and then shifting authority for goal completion to that member or members. We call the members who have been tasked with accomplishing these subgoals the *goal leaders*. Because members hold widely different assumptions about the notion of authority, we suggest that teams explicitly define the expectations and parameters for that transfer of authority for goal completion. The goal leader, in turn, will assign tasks to other members of the team and elicit the support of others essential to carrying out the goal.

This technique, called *accountability charting*, has been adopted from the work of Beckhard and Harris (Beckhard, 1997, p. 176). In this process, the goal leader and others whose roles interrelate formulate a list of actions, decisions, and activities with respect to accomplishing the goal. These activities may include collecting data, communicating with stakeholders, developing budgets, allocating resources, or running a pilot project.

The list of the team's activities is recorded on the vertical axis of the accountability chart. Then, the team agrees upon who will be involved in each action or decision, and they list these people on the horizontal axis of the chart (see Figure 2.4).

People involved may include the following:

❖ Team members

❖ Leaders to whom the team reports (team sponsors)

❖ Customers or suppliers of the team

❖ Other individuals or teams directly involved in the decisions or who will be impacted in some way

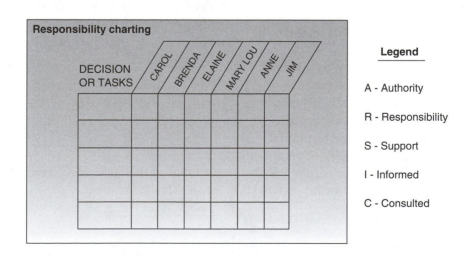

Figure 2.4   Creating Goals and Accountabilities

Next, the participants negotiate and chart the appropriate roles of each person with regard to each action or decision using the following criteria:

A—Has the authority to make decisions

R—Has the responsibility for a particular action (but not necessarily authority)

S—Has a support role; must provide resources for the action

I—Must be informed before the action

C—Must be consulted before the action

This exercise not only helps define accountabilities, but also helps clarify roles. Ambiguity regarding what one member perceives his or her role to be and how other team members perceive that role can cause considerable confusion and even conflict between members. For team effectiveness, all team members must be clear as to their roles, functions, and relationships to others both within and external to the group.

Team Fitness Exercise

Refer to Developing Clear, Motivating Goals and Accountabilities on page 126 to lead the team through the goal setting and accountability charting process.

Planner Element #4: Identifying Your Authority and Reporting Structure

The Big Question: Who has authority?
Closely linked with the development of the team's purpose is the determination of the team's boundaries for responsibility, authority, and reporting requirements. Self-managing teams will be given great latitude to decide their purpose, goals, and work methods. Most teams, however, begin with partial authority and therefore require close communication with higher management as key decisions are made.

Teams that do not have clear scope and boundaries may experience great confusion, frustration, and disappointment as they learn the hard way that they have overstepped their limits or not met their obligations. Unfortunately, this mismatch occurs often, as the concept of authority in organizations is laden with assumptions. Some people crave it, while others fear it.

The traditional and still widely held concept of authority in organizations is that it is rightly held by top management; only they have the perspective, expertise, and know-how to make good decisions. A major problem with this assumption is that with authority comes accountability, so ultimately only the most senior leaders in an organization are accountable.

With the focus on customer service and higher quality, it is fashionable to turn the organizational hierarchy upside down so that the employees who are doing the work and dealing with the customers are empowered to solve the customers' problems. Unfortunately, many organizations do not help their employees learn to take power and control. As employees make mistakes, power is pulled back from them, resulting in confusion and frustration over the concept.

To avoid these unfortunate occurrences, everyone needs to discuss and understand the following:

> ### Authority and Reporting: What Not to Do
>
> A team spent months developing a customer service protocol for answering the telephones. After conducting focus groups and surveys with their customers and arriving at a new policy for telephone etiquette, the team discovered that their senior managers were about to install a voice mail system that would make their protocol irrelevant. The senior managers, impatient with the team's progress, yanked the project back and imposed their own solution. Interviews with the team members following this fiasco revealed that some felt excluded and foolish, while others felt angry or resigned.

❖ What is the overall purpose of the team?

❖ Who specifically does the team report to?

❖ What is the scope of their mandate?

❖ In what areas does the team have full authority to make autonomous decisions?

❖ In what areas must the team consult with others?

❖ In what areas must the team refer decisions to others?

❖ What boundaries or givens—such as policies, resource constraints, and practices—must the team adhere to?

❖ With respect to the team's overall goal, does the organization expect a decision, a recommendation, information, or compliance?

The goal, of course, is to work toward more authority and accountability. We believe that if teams are to be used at all, it is important that they begin with at least enough authority to determine their own goals, work methods, and norms of conduct.

As teams mature and gain both competence and confidence, the scope of their authority should be increased. Teams need to learn together by articulating goals, experimenting with options, taking action, implementing solutions, and reflecting on their successes and failures. Through this action learning process, teams become more able and willing to assume greater levels of responsibility over time. Thus, collective responsibility for production processes, people management issues, and quality control all have a self-supporting effect on teams (Wellins, Byham, & Wilson, 1993).

In summary, by specifically defining the team's authority and then holding members accountable, members learn to work out the answers to their obligations. This strategy encourages learning and growth of team members.

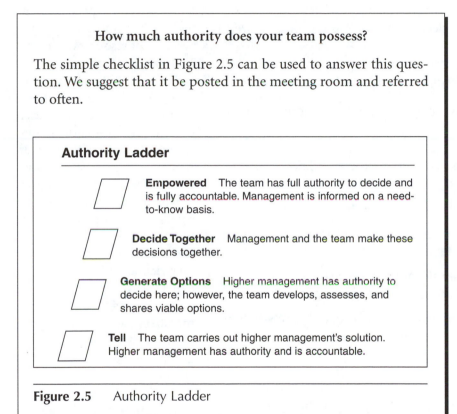

How much authority does your team possess?

The simple checklist in Figure 2.5 can be used to answer this question. We suggest that it be posted in the meeting room and referred to often.

Authority Ladder

Empowered   The team has full authority to decide and is fully accountable. Management is informed on a need-to-know basis.

Decide Together   Management and the team make these decisions together.

Generate Options   Higher management has authority to decide here; however, the team develops, assesses, and shares viable options.

Tell   The team carries out higher management's solution. Higher management has authority and is accountable.

Figure 2.5   Authority Ladder

TEAM FITNESS EXERCISE

For a team to be accountable, it must have the necessary resources such as information, budget, and time, as well as the support of internal suppliers and stakeholders. The Negotiating Authority With Your Team Sponsor exercise on page 130 is a useful tool for clarifying a team's level of authority and for identifying the resources and the support it needs to successfully accomplish its goals.

SOCIAL PROCESSES: FOSTERING GOOD RELATIONSHIPS

Planner Element #5: Establishing Team Membership and Contribution

The Big Question: Who is part of the team and who does what?

Part A: Membership—The Makeup of a Smart Team

A critical issue for team success is team membership, having the right mix of skills, experience, and leadership to ensure that the team can deliver on its performance expectations. With purpose, process, and expected results clearly defined, it is a good practice to review team membership for the best mix of resources and optimal size (see Figure 2.6).

If the team's goals are complex, requiring team members to problem-solve and reach consensus on major issues, teams of about six or seven members are most effective. Our research indicates that performance declines in smaller teams of two or three members, probably because teams do not have the necessary richness of experience or expertise to draw from. In larger teams (10 or more members), group satisfaction declines. It seems that as the group size becomes too large, both interaction and communication tend to become difficult, resulting in dissatisfied members and unproductive interactions.

Team designers can take comfort from another major finding from our research. With one small exception, we found no significant effect on performance from demographic or personality variables. In other words, don't

---

Who should the optimal team include?

Generally, team membership should include individuals who

- ❖ possess critical expertise, knowledge, or information for the tasks at hand;

- ❖ have a stake in the final outcome;

- ❖ have responsibility for implementing whatever is decided;

- ❖ have relevant and diverse viewpoints that will stimulate discussion and thinking;

- ❖ have the authority to decide on behalf of their constituents.

Often, due to time and size constraints, the formal team cannot include all relevant individuals. In these cases, creativity is required to find ways to bring necessary insights and perspectives to the team. Teams can invite subject matter experts or key customers to provide briefings, can form advisory boards composed of relevant stakeholder groups to impart feedback, can hold town hall meetings, or can run a series of focus sessions. What's important is that the team invite essential others to participate.

worry about balancing the team with respect to age, gender, personality type, thinking styles, or other personality variables. Developing the team skills described in this guide is much more important. These skills will help you harness the creative friction that naturally occurs from the diversity of any group.

The one small exception? Teams will not benefit from the loner who does not like working in a group and who will not abide by the team's norms and processes. That person is a negative. But don't worry: Our research shows that there are not many lone wolves out there.

Using an Advisory Community to Inform the Team

A team of administrators and principals at a local school district wanted input from the wider school community on their vision for the future. To accomplish this critical input, their eight-person team used a 70-member Advisory Community composed of educators, parents, students, union officials, clergy, community members, staff, trustees, and academics. The Advisory Community was involved in three one-day meetings to help create, refine, and approve the vision.

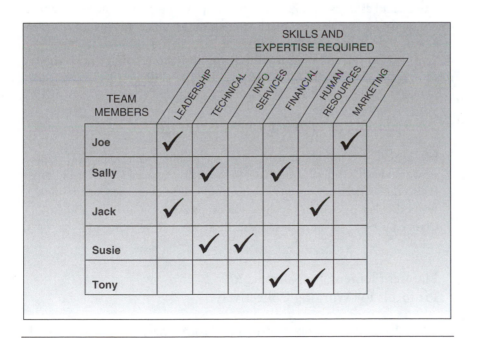

TEAM MEMBERS	LEADERSHIP	TECHNICAL	INFO SERVICES	FINANCIAL	HUMAN RESOURCES	MARKETING
Joe	✓					✓
Sally		✓		✓		
Jack	✓				✓	
Susie		✓	✓			
Tony				✓	✓	

Figure 2.6   Team Member Selection Guide

TEAM FITNESS EXERCISE

Refer to Defining Team Membership and Contribution on page 132 to ensure that your team has the right composition.

Part B: Contributions—Using the
Talents of All Team Members to Achieve Synergy

While having the right membership mix on a team is necessary, it does not guarantee that members will recognize and fully utilize the talents of all team members. What is critically important is that each member's talents are tapped and work is allocated according to member talents and abilities.

Carol likes to tell the story of an experience she had while facilitating the popular exercise Subarctic Survival with an MBA class. In Subarctic Survival, team members stranded in a dangerous environment are asked to rank a list of supplies in terms of their importance to the group's survival. To win the game, or survive, members must pool their knowledge of the Arctic to select the supplies that will keep them alive until help arrives. Members rank the items individually first, and then as a group. Next, the group determines whether its group score is better than the averaged individual scores. If the group score is higher, the team has achieved a synergy gain.

On this occasion, the team included a young Native American man who quite naturally possessed expertise on surviving in the Subarctic. However, his fellow MBA teammates did not recognize or accept his advice or perspectives, and as a result, the team ended up with a score much lower than the score the young Native American man obtained on his own. This exercise was a striking example of how teams can reject critical input and insights—a powerful lesson for the team and the whole class about the need to respect and build on member talents to achieve a collective gain.

TEAM FITNESS EXERCISE

See Defining Team Membership and Contribution on page 132 and Resources Each Member Contributes to the Team on page 135. Contribution is also closely related to norms for inclusion and roles and accountabilities. For a detailed discussion on these topics, please refer to Roles and Role Clarity on page 41 and Norms and Protocols for Working Collectively below.

Planner Element #6: Norms and Protocols for Working Collectively

The Big Questions: How do we do things around here? How should we do things around here?"

A professor friend of ours jokingly compared the process of making decisions at meetings with his academic colleagues to the process of trying to herd a group of cats. This experience may sound familiar. When people get together in a group to make decisions, they need norms and protocols to structure their thinking and participation as they collect data, make sense of the data, and come to conclusions.

The problem with our academic group is that they had no helpful norms or protocols for sharing information and making decisions. They had fallen into the all-too-familiar trap of assuming that every decision needs to be made by consensus. In reality, some decisions are best made individually or by a small group and then shared with and tested by the larger group.

Consensus is reached when each member of the team is willing to commit to the decision or product and each member is willing to commit to actions for implementing the solution. In reaching consensus, the process the team adopts in researching and analyzing the challenge and exploring options is just as important as the solution itself.

> Team consensus is preferable when the team is tasked with a relevant challenge that all members need to accept (Maier, 1963) and when the process for reaching a decision is just as important as the decision (Harrington-Mackin, 1994).

When members together (a) collect and analyze key data to explore the challenge, (b) analyze the data from many relevant perspectives, (c) seek feedback and advice from important stakeholders, and (d) test their solutions via prototypes, pilots, and focus groups, they will necessarily develop a joint appreciation for the complexities of the challenge, and the preferable options will emerge. In short, consensus comes from doing the work.

What sets smart teams apart from others is not which decision tools they use, but that they discuss and agree on norms and protocols for important aspects of working collectively. Norms are those consistent and enduring behaviors that group members have explicitly or implicitly agreed to. They support a set of shared beliefs, values, and expectations for team behaviors and determine "how we do things around here."

It is important for teams to understand that if helpful norms are not explicitly defined, unhelpful norms may implicitly emerge. Implicit or explicit, some group's norms help by fostering interaction and effective decision making, while some hinder performance by preventing dialogue or promoting premature decision making. To test this concept, think of the norms, both helpful and hindering, that a team you belonged to has sanctioned. Do they allow members to hold side conversations? Do they permit member tardiness at meetings? Do they allow members to veer the discussion off track? All of these norms are examples of hindering behaviors, which, although frustrating, are implicitly sanctioned when the team does not address or correct them. So whether team norms are functional or dysfunctional, they are the accepted behaviors by which the team operates.

Agreeing to a few explicit and helpful norms for group work early in a team's life is important, as they help members think through and define their ideal behavioral expectations for each other. Members feel empowered to create their ideal team environment and processes for group work. In essence, they create a sense of security that they will be valued and included and that processes will be used to manage conflict, solve problems, and make decisions.

DEVELOPING PROTOCOLS
FOR TEAM PROBLEM SOLVING

Although there are many problem-solving processes available, most are built on the following fundamentals: problem identification and description, problem analysis, option generation, solution selection, action planning, and follow through. Our adaptation of the problem-solving process, complete with tools and techniques for generating powerful team solutions to complex problems, is found in Chapter 3.

DEVELOPING PROTOCOLS
FOR HANDLING CONFLICT

From time to time, most teams will experience conflict that gets in the way of team progress. Often, the conflict occurs due to a misunderstanding, or members may have different values, mindsets, or working styles. If these tensions are left unchecked, members tend to act out their feelings, resulting in destructive behaviors such as discounting member input, emotional outbursts, or the formation of cliques.

Teams that are skilled at conflict handling stave off this destructive conflict by creating norms for welcoming diverse views, accepting controversial statements, and openly sharing feelings. When teams ask for and encourage—yes, we said encourage—members to offer controversial opinions, a climate of openness and exploration is created. We believe that this norm is the most critical factor in helping teams stay focused and on track (Weisbord & Janoff, 1995).

Next, when conflict stops the group from working constructively, members pause to ask why. Developing a group norm for surfacing thorny issues as they occur, as well as examining ways the team can prevent them, is always advisable. Having regular "check-ins" and evaluations of how the team is working together will also go a long way toward creating honest and healthy relationships. From time to time, members need the opportunity to share their feelings and needs in a safe way.

To be useful, norms and protocols should continue to evolve, as members discover what behaviors and processes are truly important for working together effectively. With each successive iteration, the list of norms and protocols will become smaller but will have more impact, as teams narrow down the behaviors and approaches that are truly helpful.

For more information, refer to Chapter 4, "Handling Team Conflict."

TEAM FITNESS EXERCISES

To give team members the opportunity and permission to talk about how they think good team members should behave, refer to the Team Culture Audit on page 137. To begin your team's discussion of useful norms and protocols, refer to Creating Helpful Norms and Protocols on page 186.

Planner Element #7: Roles and Role Clarity

The Big Question: How will each member contribute?

When a team is formed, each member is faced with questions about his or her role: Why am I here? What do people expect from me? How will I contribute? Clarifying support roles for effective team meetings helps keep members focused and productive. (See Figure 2.7.)

ω *Facilitator:* designs meetings to ensure that people have the right conversations to move forward

ω *Scribe:* records ideas on a flipchart to make sure that ideas do not get lost; provides members with a record of key items discussed, decisions made, and commitments

ω *Timekeeper:* helps the facilitator track the time to ensure the work gets done in the time allotted

ω *Coach:* person with expertise and/or political clout to assist the team as needed

---

Figure 2.7   Roles for Team Management

Team Leader/Facilitator

As ringleader, guide, process expert, and catalyst, the team leader has a critical role. Ever mindful of both the task and social complexities, the team leader is three parts process facilitator and one part project manager, as follows:

Leader as Facilitator

❖ Leads the team through a series of exercises and questions to co-create their Team Management Practices

❖ Plans and facilitates an agenda to ensure that members jointly share, analyze, and evaluate data for synergistic decision making

❖ Provides an overall roadmap for the group's approach to working together, making sure to match the challenge at hand with the appropriate tools and technologies

❖ Encourages balanced participation by creating a safe climate and protecting ideas

❖ Helps members work through differences of opinion constructively

❖ Assists the team in addressing counterproductive behaviors

❖ Leads the team in developing and using group norms to guide behavior

❖ Ensures that team members understand their roles and responsibilities

❖ Keeps team meetings focused and productive

❖ Ensures that relevant information is available for the team's deliberations

❖ Invites experts to team meetings to supplement the team's collective knowledge and experience

❖ Checks for comprehension and understanding

❖ Provides feedback to team members

❖ Asks effective questions

❖ Develops team members and encourages shared team leadership

Leader as Project Manager

❖ Schedules, arranges, and facilitates team meetings

❖ Clarifies purpose and team goals

❖ Summarizes and organizes ideas, checks for understanding and commitment, and assigns tasks

❖ Ensures that the team uses agreed-upon problem-solving methods

❖ Ensures that action items are assigned and follows up to ensure completion

❖ Keeps the team coach and management apprised of team progress and issues

A major goal for self-managing teams is to share leadership responsibilities among the full team. As the team develops and matures, members can and will gradually assume more responsibility for these roles.

Scribe

The team leader is often too busy wearing his or her "task" and "group process" hats to record group discussion and decisions. As such, a scribe or recorder should be appointed before each team meeting to take and distribute the minutes to team members. We recommend that the scribe capture only the relevant data, including the meeting's purpose, relevant discussion themes, points of agreement and disagreement, decisions for action, and accountabilities.

A useful form for taking team minutes is shown in Figure 2.8.

Notes From Our Team Meeting

Date:

Attendance:

Topic:

Discussion (discussion and points of agreement and disagreement):

Decisions (including timing and accountabilities):

Responsibilities:

_____

_____

Figure 2.8   Team Notes Form

Timekeeper

The role of the timekeeper is to alert the team several minutes prior to the end of the time limit for each agenda item. The timekeeper's role is not to move the group to the next agenda item when the time limit is up. Rather, if an agenda item requires further time, the team will decide to either spend the required time to complete the agenda item or close the agenda item for completion at another time.

Team Members

Effective team members are committed team members. That means they "show up" and participate enthusiastically throughout the team's life cycle. While good team management practices will help to build the necessary commitment, every member must personally agree to invest in the team by agreeing to

- ❖ prepare prior to the meetings;
- ❖ attend team meetings on time for the full meeting;
- ❖ participate fully by providing key information, voicing opinions, and listening actively;
- ❖ accept and complete work assignments set by the team;
- ❖ serve as facilitator, scribe, timekeeper, and process advisor as needed;
- ❖ accept and support consensus decisions of the team.

Team Coach/Advisor

Newly formed teams can benefit greatly from the support of a team coach. The coach is not a member of the team but rather a resource assigned to the team to assist with solving political issues, opening communication channels with key stakeholder groups, and testing or refining ideas before they are shared widely.

The role of the coach is to

- ❖ provide guidance, advice, and development for the team, primarily by coaching the team leader;
- ❖ when called upon by the team, act as team ambassador and communication link with senior management to remove barriers (e.g., political, procedural, resource related) to team success;
- ❖ offer guidance on how to manage political issues, should they occur.

Thus, it is not the role of the coach to meddle with internal team dynamics. Rather, appropriate interventions focus on support issues, such as communicating with upper management and removing barriers outside of the team's authority. At the same time, the coach should never let a flailing team fail. Such behavior is not supportive or constructive.

It is very important for the coach to respect the authority of the team. The coach/advisor is a team resource, not a team member or team decision maker. The coach is not responsible for team results, the team is.

Planner Element #8: Developing Relationships and Communications

The Big Question: Who else needs to be committed to our initiative to make it happen?

A group is not an island unto itself. Most groups cannot survive without the assistance and support of other individuals and groups within the organization. Teams who view themselves as part of the larger organization are acutely aware of the web of interrelationships that they must develop to achieve their goals. These interrelationships provide the team with important information and feedback, which helps them stay aligned with the overall priorities and goals of the organization.

At the earliest stage in a team's development, members need to identify the key people and groups who have a stake in the challenge, as well as how these key stakeholders will be informed, involved, and consulted. Involving key stakeholders early will ensure that important perspectives, information, and expertise are carefully considered so that smart, workable solutions are adopted and supported. Stakeholder mapping is a useful tool for this important dialogue.

Stakeholder mapping involves brainstorming the key relationships that need to be managed for your team initiative to be a success. These people and groups are listed in the second circle in Figure 2.9. Next, participants identify processes and systems that will be impacted by the team initiative and record them in the outer circle.

> **How do we build relationships and partner with our key stakeholders? By asking questions such as the following:**
>
> ❖ Who are our key stakeholders?
>
> ❖ What do we need to know from them? What do they need to know from us?
>
> ❖ What joint goals do we have in common?
>
> ❖ How will we work together to achieve those joint goals?
>
> ❖ Who specifically is responsible and accountable for carrying out activities toward our joint goals?
>
> ❖ When issues arise or disagreements occur, how will we resolve them?
>
> ❖ What will our norms and protocols be for working together?
>
> ❖ How will we communicate our progress and issues to the organization and our customers?
>
> ❖ What organizational processes, policies, and protocols are we bound by? What processes, policies, and protocols are we free to change?
>
> ❖ In what ways can we align and improve our processes to create synergy?

The team now has a map of the processes and systems they will need to address with key stakeholders.

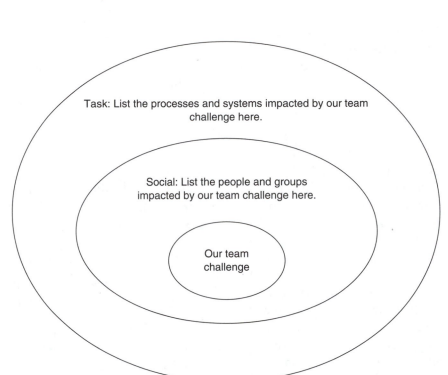

Figure 2.9   Stakeholder Mapping

This simple clarification can provide great leverage for cooperation and alignment between teams. For example, a Product Sourcing team in a manufacturing environment found their efforts constantly thwarted by a Marketing team located 155 miles away in the organization's corporate head office. The two teams were working at cross-purposes; Marketing was promising product to the retail chain before the Sourcing team could reasonably guarantee the product. The two teams had not taken the time to identify joint goals or discuss what they needed from each other to satisfy Sourcing's product quality requirements and Marketing's need to put the product on the shelves of retail outlets.

To address this challenge, the teams scheduled a facilitated partnering session to clarify their overlapping goals, processes, and responsibilities. The session began an ongoing dialogue that helped each team better understand the pressures and constraints of the other. This ultimately led to better planning processes, more cross-functional meetings, a clarification of roles and responsibilities, and the elimination of several procedural barriers. The result was a drastic improvement in customer service to the retail chain and, just as importantly, in the relationship between Marketing and Sourcing.

We highly recommend that teams invite key stakeholders, such as their executive sponsors, to work through the Team Management Practices Planner with them. After all, teams can only benefit from having in-depth discussions with those who have a vested interest in their success. And what better way to form and strengthen these important relationships as soon as the team is formed?

Stakeholders will provide important information, perspectives, and insight on most aspects of the planning process, such as the team's mission and scope. For example, an executive sponsor will be able to help focus the team on its specific purpose, clarify questions regarding the group's authority, approve membership requirements, and remove barriers in the team's path.

Moreover, working through the Planner is a commitment-building process. Involving key stakeholders will help build necessary support for the team and ensure that the team's goals are fully aligned with the super-ordinate goals of the organization. This alignment occurs as the team and its stakeholders develop the fine details between stakeholder expectations and what the team can actually accomplish given its membership, resources, and authority.

In addition, stakeholders involved in defining the team's mission, goals, scope, membership, authority, and expected results will understand the full extent of the team's challenges and their role in helping the team achieve its goals. So often we hear teams complain that their executive sponsors expect them to accomplish unrealistic goals within impossible timelines and under severe resource constraints. Or they complain that they do not have necessary support from other teams and functions. If stakeholders of a team are not aligned with the mission and goals of a team, they may not place a high priority on satisfying the team's needs.

It is important to note that the executive sponsor and other stakeholders are not team members per se. Rather, they are invited guests providing important and critical input, not members with veto or decision-making power during team discussions. Executive sponsors and stakeholders must realize that if they violate these boundaries, they risk either being excluded from the team's decision making or subverting the team's work.

For a detailed description of senior management's role in fostering an optimal environment for teams, turn to Chapter 5: "Fostering a Supportive Infrastructure for Teams."

COMMITMENT PROCESS:
MAINTAINING TEAM ENERGY AND FOCUS

Planner Element #9: Results and Reflection

The Big Question: How do we reinvent our team management practices as we develop?

There are many occasions when standing back and reflecting on a situation promotes the deepest learning. Most teams are too busy doing their work to consider how well they are performing or whether they are abiding by their protocols for decision making and social inclusion. From time to time, it is extremely helpful for the team to stop and think about these issues.

Evaluation: The Lesson of the Climbing Gym

Brenda took her 6-year-old son to the wall climbing gym. Although not an expert wall climber, she was able to see potential moves up the wall that he was not able to see because he was too close to the situation. Nose to the wall, hands and feet firmly gripping the holds, it required all of his strength and energy to hold on. Standing well back, she was able to point out possible moves, which he was then able to expertly adopt. After reversing roles, she quickly realized how much strength and skill it took to reach the top, and she too was very thankful for helpful feedback from the floor below.

It doesn't matter how the team reflects on its working patterns: For example, some teams like to schedule a mini retreat to assess and refresh, while other teams like to set aside time at the end of each meeting. Independent of the venue, the evaluation session should uncover what *thinking and actions* helped the group move forward and what *thinking and actions* blocked the group from moving forward. The group can then discuss what actions and processes they will adopt to help them in the future. Toward this end, the Team Effectiveness Gap Analyzer (refer to page 12) may help the team reexamine how their critical task, social, and commitment processes can be strengthened to enhance performance.

It is important to note that evaluating team effectiveness requires that members be willing to candidly share how they are feeling about their personal experiences as a member of the team. Members must also be willing to accept feedback about how their own actions were interpreted by the group. It is critical that the facilitator approach the evaluation from a learning point of view, encouraging members to be sensitive and caring.

When members approach the giving and receiving of feedback from the perspective of "I'm okay and so are you," the feedback is targeted to the situation, issue, or behavior and not on the personality of members themselves. From this safe base, members can take responsibility for adapting their behaviors to improve team sharing and performance.

TEAM FITNESS EXERCISES

The Team Effectiveness Model Gap Analyzer (page 12), the Team Management Practices Assessment (page 117), the Problem-Solving Assessment (page 145), and the Handling Problems in Team Discussion Assessment (page 182) all allow the team to monitor its progress in key areas for team effectiveness and consider actions for improvement.

Sample Team Evaluation Agenda

1. Review ground rules. Discuss how well the group has been adhering to the ground rules. What do we need to do more of, do less of, and continue to do because it is really working? Refine your ground rules to accommodate your new thinking.

2. Review team successes. What thinking and behaviors helped us achieve this success? As a result of this discussion, what do we need to do more of and less of? What more is left to do? Incorporate this feedback into your team action plans, norms, or processes.

3. Review areas where the team has not been successful. What thinking and behaviors blocked our team from accomplishing our goals? As a result of this discussion, what do we need to do more of and less of? What do we need to stop doing altogether? How will we incorporate these realizations into team goals, norms, or processes?

Here are two final thoughts for senior managers and team sponsors to keep in mind while creating team management practices.

Senior managers: Stay at 30,000 feet; the view is better. Senior management teams creating their team management practices often fall into the trap of focusing on the challenges and priorities of each leader's department and not on the challenges that they need to tackle jointly. This distinction is subtle yet critical. If the top team's focus is on the former, their output will naturally default to reporting on individual department activities. To help top teams focus on the essential strategies and goals for organization-wide success, gently refocus the discussion using the following big questions: As a top team, what do you need to accomplish together? Why? What are the specific systemwide results that you will undertake and hold yourselves accountable for? What goals will you and/or your direct reports commit to doing to fulfill these systemwide goals? How do your department-wide goals need to be aligned to support these systemwide objectives?

Team sponsors: You should expect learning delays. As we discussed earlier, real teamwork takes time. Teams often report that they are held to unrealistic performance schedules by well-meaning yet counterproductive sponsors. While timelines help teams focus on priorities, teams need time for critical discovery, relationship building, data collection, analysis, and so on. As teams learn to work together and try out new processes and tools, there will be learning delays and quite possibly performance dips. Team sponsors and customers need to support the team's learning and resist putting unrealistic time pressures on the group. Arbitrary time pressures will create only a sense of frustration and diminished commitment.

Team Problem Solving for Pros 3

IN THIS CHAPTER

❖ Team Problem Solving: Signpost #2 of Team Success

❖ What Confounds Successful Problem Solving? Thinking Traps and Biases
- Group Pressures to Conform That Sideline Creativity
  The Abilene Paradox
  The Asch Experiments
  Groupthink
- Decision Biases That Throw Teams Off Track
  Status Quo Trap
  Confirming-Evidence Trap

❖ What Supports Problem-Solving Prowess? Introducing Our Model
- The Model: Three Key Skills of Expert Problem Solvers
  Problem-Solving Skill #1: Communications Patience
  Problem-Solving Skill #2: Synergy Creation
  Problem-Solving Skill #3: Disciplined Use of a Problem-Solving Process

---

Team Problem Solving: Signpost #2 of Team Success

Problem solving, the ability of team members to develop creative solutions to pressing organizational challenges, is at the core of a team's activities. Our research shows that a team's problem-solving abilities— its ability to identify the right problem, generate many ideas, build on those ideas, test them out, and implement the feasible ones—is one of the most important predictors of team success. Simply put, when teams use systematic processes and skills to enhance the quality of their thinking, they increase their "team IQ."

There is no doubt that teams are required to think smarter these days. Increasingly, teams are tasked with ambiguous dilemmas that have no clear answers or proven paths for success. More and more teams are finding that solutions that worked yesterday will not work tomorrow, or even today (refer to Chapter 1 for a detailed description of *jamais vu* versus *déjà vu* challenges). As such, team members are often required to go beyond incremental improvements to produce truly creative results.

So how do you generate the conditions for creative problem solving? Our problem-solving skills and processes are aimed at improving the way members communicate to combine their diverse knowledge and enhance the quality of their thinking.

Teams can provide the perfect breeding ground for creative, breakthrough results. Effective team management practices ensure that teams are set up with the right members with sufficient expertise and motivation to tackle the creative challenge. Add in problem-solving skills and we have all the ingredients necessary to harness members' talents and expand their thinking.

While imaginative, flexible, inclusive thinking is the ideal, we've all experienced situations in which team members stifle or reject ideas that clash with their own. We've seen the strategist dismissing the idealist, the idea person dismissing the logistics guru, and the thinker dismissing the feeler. Interestingly, studies have shown that group members actually communicate more with others who hold contrary views. Unfortunately, their communication is aimed at persuading those other members to adopt their views (studies reported by Festinger, Schachter, & Back, 1950). In

---

All in a Stew: The Right Mixture for Creative Problem Solving

Harvard's Teresa Amabile (1999) likens creative problem solving to making a good stew. It requires the combination of three essential ingredients: expertise, the ability to think innovatively, and the motivation to excel. The first essential ingredient, like the meat and vegetables of the stew, is expertise in a certain domain. "No one is going to do anything creative in nuclear physics unless that person knows something—and probably a great deal—about nuclear physics," says Amabile. "The ingredients of creativity start with skill in the domain—with the expertise."

The second essential ingredient is the ability to think flexibly and imaginatively. According to Amabile, "These are like the spices and herbs you use to bring out the flavor of the basic ingredients of the stew." The final ingredient is a motivation or deep commitment to confront the challenge for the pure pleasure of the pursuit. A committed group of people, compelled to solve a challenge, "is like the fire underneath the stew pot," says Amabile.

other words, much of the effort in group communications can go into convincing and dismissing and not into listening, understanding, and learning.

Teams that accept and encourage the diversity that naturally occurs among members can learn from each other's natural working styles and biases, but they must also avoid thinking traps that narrow the ideas they entertain. Next we will examine some of the social pressures and thinking traps that team members may fall into if they do not follow disciplined problem-solving processes. These traps are dangerous in that they limit real involvement and stifle creativity.

What Confounds Successful Problem Solving? Thinking Traps and Biases

Team members not only must overcome difficulties arising from diverse working styles and biases but also must avoid thinking traps that narrow the ideas they entertain.

These well-documented psychological traps take several forms, including decision biases, misperceptions, unchecked assumptions, and social pressures. What makes these traps so dangerous is that they are often invisible to members.

The result of group pressures and decision-making traps is rather obvious. Poor decision-making practices lead to poor and often inadequate decisions. Groups experiencing some or all of these symptoms do not generate creative ideas; rather, they limit their analysis to a few narrow preselected options. These options are not tested or evaluated but instead are protected or prematurely discarded. Members make little or no attempt to collect crucial data, expert opinion, or feedback from important stakeholders. Moreover, data that support their initial view are given great weight, whereas data that are in conflict with their initial views are discounted.

Let's examine some of these issues that limit team problem-solving proficiency.

GROUP PRESSURES TO CONFORM THAT SIDELINE CREATIVITY

The Abilene Paradox: Beware Counterproductive Team Agreement

Jerry Harvey (1988) coined the expression "Abilene Paradox" to describe a dynamic whereby the group's inability to manage agreement produces faulty decisions. That's right; it is the group's failure to manage *agreement*—not disagreement—that gets members into trouble. As you will see from Harvey's colorful depiction, group members tend to take trips to places they don't want to go, simply to fulfill their need to belong.

According to Harvey, groups that fail to manage agreement display the following characteristics. First, individual members agree on the nature of the problem or the preferred action. However, because members fail to communicate their desires and beliefs, they make a collective decision that no member truly supports. As a result, the group's actions are counter-productive. Next comes the blaming. As members become frustrated, angry, and irritated from taking an action they truly didn't support, they direct their aggression at each other. The result? No accountability, no commitment, no team. Harvey believes that groups can become perpetual travelers to Abilene and warns that groups that do not learn to manage agreement will have a one-way ticket.

The Abilene Paradox: The Management of Agreement

That July afternoon in Coleman, Texas (population 5,607), was particularly hot—104 degrees according to the Walgreen's Rexall thermometer. In addition, the wind was blowing fine-grained West Texas topsoil through the house. But the afternoon was still tolerable—even potentially enjoyable. A fan was stirring the air on the back porch; there was cold lemonade; and finally, there was entertainment. Dominoes. Perfect for the conditions. The game requires little more physical exertion than an occasional mumbled comment, "Shuffle 'em," and an unhurried movement of the arm to place the tiles in their appropriate positions on the table. All in all, it had the makings of an agreeable Sunday afternoon in Coleman. That is, until my father-in-law suddenly said, "Let's get in the car and go to Abilene and have dinner at the cafeteria."

I thought, "What, go to Abilene? Fifty-three miles? In this dust storm and heat? And in an unairconditioned 1958 Buick?"

But my wife chimed in with, "Sounds like a great idea. I'd like to go. How about you, Jerry?" Since my own preferences were obviously out of step with the rest, I replied, "Sounds good to me," and added, "I just hope your mother wants to go."

"Of course I want to go," said my mother-in-law. "I haven't been to Abilene in a long time." So into the car and off to Abilene we went. My predictions were fulfilled. The heat was brutal. Perspiration had cemented a fine layer of dust on our skin by the time we arrived. The cafeteria's food could serve as a first-rate prop in an antacid commercial.

Some four to six hours and 106 miles later, we returned to Coleman, hot and exhausted. We silently sat in front of the fan for a long time. Then, to be sociable and to break the silence, I dishonestly said, "It was a great trip, wasn't it?"

No one spoke.

Finally, my mother-in-law said, with some irritation, "Well, to tell the truth, I really didn't enjoy it much and would rather have stayed here. I just went along because the three of you were so enthusiastic about going. I wouldn't have gone if you all hadn't pressured me into it."

I couldn't believe it. "What do you mean 'you all'?" I said. "Don't put me in the 'you all' group. I was delighted to be doing what we were doing. I didn't want to go. I only went to satisfy the rest of you. You're the culprits."

My wife looked shocked. "Don't call me a culprit. You and Daddy and Mama were the ones who wanted to go. I just went along to keep you happy. I would have had to be crazy to want to go out in heat like that." Her father entered the conversation with one word: "Shee-it." He then expanded on what was already absolutely clear: "Listen, I never wanted to go to Abilene. I just thought you might be bored. You visit so seldom I wanted to be sure you enjoyed it. I would have preferred to play another game of dominoes and eat leftovers in the icebox."

After the outburst of recrimination, we all sat back in silence. Here we were, four reasonably sensible people who—of our own volition—had just taken a 106-mile trip across a godforsaken desert in furnace-like heat and a dust storm to eat unpalatable food at a hole-in-the-wall cafeteria in Abilene, when none of us had really wanted to go. To be concise, we'd done just the opposite of what we wanted to do. The whole situation simply didn't make sense.

From Harvey, J. B., *Abilene Paradox & Other Meditations on Management.* Copyright © 1988. This material is used by permission of John Wiley and Sons, Inc.

The Asch Experiments:
Creating Conditions for Real Involvement

Social psychologist Solomon Asch was a pioneer in the study of how group pressure impacts group decision making. Through a series of carefully constructed experiments, he contributed greatly to our understanding of how social and personal conditions cause individuals to resist or yield to group pressures.

In his most famous set of experiments, Asch asked participants (seven confederates who were secretly cooperating with the experimenter and one unsuspecting subject) to compare a line drawn on a standard card with three lines of varying lengths drawn on a comparison card. The participants were asked to select the line on the comparison card that was identical to the line on the standard card. The subjects played 12 rounds in all.

For the first two rounds, the confederates were instructed to offer the correct answer and so all participants were in agreement. In the next rounds, however, the confederates were instructed to answer incorrectly. As a result, the unsuspecting subjects found themselves in a rather peculiar situation; their senses were telling them one thing and the group another. As Asch (1953) noted, "[H]e faced, possibly for the first time in his life, a situation in which a group unanimously contradicted the evidence of his senses."

Asch found a wide variance in how individual subjects responded. Reporting on the results of 50 unsuspecting subjects, approximately one third of the subjects went along with the group and also gave the wrong answer. Asch called this the majority effect. Another one quarter of the unsuspecting subjects remained completely independent, with the remaining subjects acquiescing with the majority on some rounds and answering independently on others (see Figure 3.1).

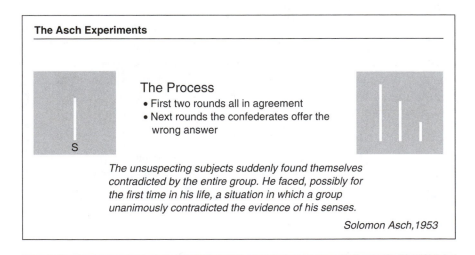

The Asch Experiments

The Process
- First two rounds all in agreement
- Next rounds the confederates offer the wrong answer

The unsuspecting subjects suddenly found themselves contradicted by the entire group. He faced, possibly for the first time in his life, a situation in which a group unanimously contradicted the evidence of his senses.

Solomon Asch, 1953

Figure 3.1   The Asch Experiments

As Asch varied the conditions of his experiments, he made many interesting discoveries. When he made the task more complex by reducing the variance of the comparison lines, the majority effect became even stronger.

However, when one or more of the confederates offered an answer that varied from the group's, the majority effect was reduced. Interestingly enough, the correctness of the dissenting confederate's decision did not matter. As long as at least one other person offered an answer that was different from the majority view, the unsuspecting subject felt confident enough to present his or her own answer. This effect was diminished when the dissenting confederate started conforming again.

In a further adaptation, Asch totally reversed the conditions for the experiment so that the uninformed subjects were the majority and the confederate was one individual who intentionally gave the wrong answer. Under these conditions, the naïve majority ostracized the confederate, smirking, laughing, and insulting him when he offered the wrong answer.

Following each experiment, the subjects were interviewed to discover why they responded the way they did. Interestingly, there was great variance among the subjects. Of those who remained independent, some were unwaveringly confident in their decisions; they knew what they saw and they held firm. Others, on the other hand, were beginning to doubt themselves and questioned the accuracy of their perceptions. Of the subjects who yielded to the majority effect, a subset truly believed that the majority estimates were correct; in their opinion, if everybody else saw it that way, it must have been true. Once again, however, a subset admitted that they simply conformed out of a need to belong and not appear to be different.

And so what can we learn from Asch's experiments, and how can we apply this wisdom to our teams? Asch (1953) concluded that there is a "fundamental psychological difference between the condition of being alone and having a minimum of human support." It seems that people are more willing to offer up what they know, see, and have learned when they sense that others are with them and will accept it. And so perhaps the greatest lesson is the simple yet profound notion that we free people to act and fully participate when we create conditions in which all members feel comfortable to express their true thoughts, feelings, and judgments—prudent advice for today's teams faced with ambiguous situations and no clear proven path or answer.

> ### Research Note:
> ### The Powers and Pressures of Belonging Versus Independence
>
> The results of the Asch experiments seem to suggest that many of us need to feel a sense of belonging before we can contribute openly and fully to collective work. We feel awkward and exposed when we stand alone. Of greatest significance, it seems that we are freer to be independent when at least one other person expresses a perspective that runs counter to the majority. Moreover, Asch found that our fears of reprisal for expressing opinions that vary significantly from the group are real, as his naïve subjects laughed and ridiculed the dissenting confederate who had intentionally given the wrong answer.

Groupthink: The Illusion of Good Decisions

Groupthink is a social condition that prevents a group from debating the real issues and critically appraising its actions. Irving Janis (1971) coined the well-known phrase after examining the decision-making dynamics of the close group of advisors to President John F. Kennedy who blundered into the Bay of Pigs invasion. After ruling out stupidity, "for the men who participated in the Bay of Pigs decision comprised great intellectual talent," Janis posited that some other factors must be at work.

So Janis looked at the fiasco from the standpoint of group dynamics. He defined *groupthink* as a way to "refer to the mode of thinking that persons engage in when *concurrence-seeking* becomes so dominant in a cohesive in-group that that it tends to override realistic appraisal of alternative courses of action" (Janis, 1971, p. 400). Simply put, while members have divergent views, they do not express them because the pressure they feel to conform is too great.

Agreement comes at the expense of analysis so as to avoid conflict and responsibility.

Testing Your Team for Groupthink: Notable Symptoms

Janis identified eight symptoms of groupthink, which are described in the following paragraphs.

Invulnerability
Most or all of the members of a group share an illusion of invulnerability, which leads to excessive optimism and encourages extreme risk taking. It also causes members to fail to respond to clear warnings of danger. "The Kennedy in-group, which uncritically accepted the Central Intelligence Agency's disastrous Bay of Pigs Plan, operated on the false assumption that they could keep secret the fact that the United States was responsible for the invasion of Cuba. Even after news of the plan began to leak out, their belief remained unshaken. They failed even to consider the danger that awaited them: a worldwide revulsion against the U.S." (Janis, 1971, p. 402).

Rationalization
Victims of groupthink ignore warnings. Collectively they rationalize and discount warnings that otherwise would lead members to reconsider their assumptions.

Morality
Victims of groupthink believe unquestionably in their inherent morality, inclining members to ignore the ethical and moral consequences of their decisions. Janis identified at least two influential people who had major misgivings with the morality of the Bay of Pigs plan. As he writes,

One of them, Arthur Schlesinger Jr., presented his strong objections in a memorandum to President Kennedy and Secretary of State Rusk, but suppressed them when he attended meetings of the Kennedy team. The other, Senator J. William Fulbright, was not a member of the group, but the President invited him to express his misgivings in a speech to the policymakers. However, when Fulbright finished speaking, the President moved on to other agenda items without asking for the reactions of the group. (p. 404)

Stereotypes

Victims of groupthink hold stereotyped views of the enemy as too evil, weak, or stupid to oppose the group's risky attempts. Kennedy's group held misguided assumptions about Fidel Castro's army, which led them to overlook the many obstacles to their plan's success. As Janis notes,

> [T]he Kennedy groupthinkers believed that Castro's air force was so ineffectual that obsolete B-26s could knock it out completely in a surprise attack before the invasion began. They also believed that Castro's army was so weak that a small Cuban-exile brigade could establish a well-protected beachhead at the Bay of Pigs. In addition, they believed that Castro was not smart enough to put down any possible internal uprisings in support of the exiles. They were wrong on all three assumptions. (Janis, 1971, p. 404)

Pressure

Victims of groupthink apply direct pressure on members who express contrary views, reinforcing the notion that loyal members are cohesive. Although President Kennedy was known to raise skeptical questions during the Bay of Pigs meetings, he allowed the CIA representatives to dominate by "permit[ting] them to give their immediate refutations in response to each tentative doubt that one of the others expressed, instead of asking whether anyone shared the doubt or wanted to pursue the implications of the new worrisome issue that had just been raised" (Janis, 1971, p. 405).

Self-Censorship

Victims of groupthink avoid deviating from what appears to be the group's consensus, causing each member to minimize the importance of his or her doubts.

Unanimity

Victims of groupthink share an illusion of unanimity, creating the false assumption that silence means consent. Janis reasoned that when a group of people who respect one another arrives at what appears to be a unanimous decision, they believe that the decision must be true and right. This reliance on the idea that *everyone feels this way so it must be right* replaces individual critical thinking and reality testing.

Mindguards

Victims of groupthink sometimes become self-appointed mindguards, protecting the group from unpopular or adverse information. Mindguards apply pressure on others—both from within and outside of the group—who disagree and effectively block their participation. Janis notes that Secretary of State Rusk functioned as a highly effective mindguard by failing to alert the group to strong objections from three "outsiders" who learned of the plan—Undersecretary of State Chester Bowles, USIA Director Edward Murrow, and Rusk's Intelligence Chief, Roger Hilsman.

DECISION BIASES THAT THROW TEAMS OFF TRACK

Apart from group pressures to conform, team members can also default to decision biases that limit their thinking. Most of these biases are the result of perceptual shortcuts that we use to manage the overwhelming amount of data that we encounter daily. While these perceptual shortcuts help us manage our day-to-day lives, they tend to limit our thinking by filtering out data and possibilities that are not familiar to us.

We present a mere sampling of the decision-making biases that have been identified by various experts. Our intent is to make you aware that these biases naturally occur in individuals and teams, with awareness being your best guide for avoiding them. For a fuller description of decision-making biases, refer to Hammond, Keeney, and Raiffa (1998). Their book was the reference for the following discussion.

Status Quo Trap

When the status quo trap is operating, we have a strong bias toward preserving the way things currently are. We believe that *the devil we know is better than the devil we don't know.*

Many experiments have shown the strong attraction people have to the status quo. For example, in one experiment, people within a group were randomly given one of two gifts of approximately the same value—half receiving a mug and the other half receiving a Swiss chocolate bar. While you might expect that about half of the subjects would have wanted to make the exchange (especially those subjects who did not receive the chocolate), only 1 in 10 actually did. The status quo had exerted its force. Other experiments have shown that the more choices subjects are given, the greater the pull the status quo has. When asked to choose between the status quo and option A or B, more people selected the status quo than when confronted with option A by itself. The researchers concluded that choosing between more alternatives requires greater effort and risk, and selecting the status quo avoids that effort.

Confirming-Evidence Trap

This trap leads us to seek out evidence that confirms our initial assumptions or decisions. We tend to give greater weight to the evidence supporting our initial views and less weight to contradictory evidence. The confirming-evidence traps also limits our approach to seeking out evidence. When this bias is operating, we tend to collect information from sources that support our views and avoid reviewing input from sources that may provide evidence to the contrary.

In one psychological study, two groups—one supporting capital punishment and one opposing it—each read two reports of carefully conducted research on the effectiveness of the death penalty as a deterrent to crime. One report concluded that the death penalty was effective and the other that it was not. The result? Both groups emphasized the information that supported their original viewpoint and actually became even more convinced of the validity of their own perspectives. Despite being exposed to solid scientific information supporting counterarguments, they automatically dismissed this conflicting information.

What Supports Problem-Solving Prowess? Introducing Our Model

We have studied a number of teams that have successfully honed a set of creative problem-solving capabilities. At the root of these skills is the ability of team members to balance their creative processes—whereby all members participate in team discussions, feel comfortable to speak their minds, and build on ideas—with the ability to produce and implement results—whereby members evaluate and agree on a course of action and move on.

Kathleen Eisenhardt of Stanford University refers to this form of team ingenuity as the ability to make *smart-fast* decisions. She deplores the habit of those North American managers who spend too much time analyzing and not enough time acting. Eisenhardt, who studies how successful organizations make fast, smart decisions, maintains that successful companies of the future will be the ones that encourage employees and teams to act and create within a few simple rules (Eisenhardt, 2000).

THE MODEL: THREE KEY SKILLS OF EXPERT PROBLEM SOLVERS

Our research and practice have identified the following three skill areas to help teams make smart decisions and implement them.

Problem-Solving Skill #1: Communications Patience

This skill includes techniques that help members share information and perspectives by working hard to understand one another and working hard to be understood. Members with controversial or divergent views are not ignored or blocked. Rather, members are careful to hear and understand all views, thus creating the necessary conditions for meaningful dialogue to occur.

Problem-Solving Skill #2: Synergy Creation

This involves techniques that equip members to expand their thinking by generating many ideas, building on those ideas, and evaluating ideas to create synergistic solutions. These skills are essential as they encourage teams to expand their thinking first to harness all of the divergent opinions, instead of jumping to any one solution prematurely.

Problem-Solving Skill #3: Disciplined Use of a Problem-Solving Process

Members become disciplined in using a systematic process for analyzing data, creating options, and evaluating and selecting preferred solutions.

True, these factors overlap, but together they account for the kind of problem-solving ingenuity that leads teams to innovative solutions. The good news is that we can all learn a repertoire of skills to enhance team problem solving. The following information will help you build excellent problem-solving techniques in your teams.

TEAM FITNESS EXERCISE

You may wish to begin on page 145 by assessing your team's problem-solving skills (Exercise 3.1, Team Problem-Solving Assessment).

Problem-Solving Skill #1: Communications Patience

Just as bumping, setting, and spiking are essential competencies for the members of a university volleyball team and skating, stick handling, and puck passing are critical skills for a professional hockey team, conversation is a core competence for high-performing work teams. The ability of members to share critical insights and perspectives to develop a joint database from which to diagnose issues and explore possibilities for action is a required capability.

Figure 3.2 lists some of the questions that define the communications patience success factor in our research. High-performance teams answered these questions in the affirmative. Take a minute to read through these questions. Now think of a team to which you belong. How might your team realistically answer these questions?

> **Patient Communicators**
>
> ❖ Work hard to make themselves understood
> ❖ Work hard to understand others
> ❖ Do not blame each other when misunderstandings occur
> ❖ Do not insist on their solutions while allowing others to sit back passively

---

Communications Patience

ω   Do we make sure that we clearly understand each other's point of view before solving problems?

ω   When we misunderstand each other, do we slow down and find a way to correct the problem?

ω   Do group members work hard for a complete understanding of the issues?

ω   When someone doesn't agree or understand, do we always find out their reasons?

ω   Do we work hard to come up with solutions acceptable to all of us?

ω   Do we bring everyone's concerns out into the open so that issues are fully explored?

Figure 3.2   Communications Patience

Chances are that your team will not have answered all of these questions in the affirmative. In our great haste to do more, faster, with less, we often speak in code with short, fast monologue replacing deep, meaningful dialogue. And so, although we know that our fellow team members do not have the capacity to actually read our minds, we often communicate with them as if they do.

Similarly, when it comes to active listening, most of us do not listen at a very deep level. We have a natural tendency to

> **So Why Don't We Listen Well?**
>
> While people spend more time listening than any other communication activity, research shows that we listen at about 25% efficiency. This is surprising when most of us report that we are good listeners.

evaluate and judge what we are hearing. When we hear another speak from their unique perspective, we typically go through a process of evaluation to determine whether we agree or disagree. Agreement usually leads to supportive gestures. Disagreement, on the other hand, leads to debate or avoidance. Either way, the conversation remains at the surface, and real shared understanding rarely develops. The result? We find ourselves participating in what Marvin Weisbord (personal communication, 2000) refers to as the *same, different* meeting. We are all in the same physical space, yet we are not connecting.

Patient communicators understand that the communications process is fraught with difficulty and that "noise" of many sorts—including time pressures, interruptions, biases, and attitudes—interferes with the ability of speakers to send messages and of listeners to receive them. Having developed an orientation that helps members slow down to fully share, explore, and digest key insights, patient communicators do not dampen passionate stances or deem them too hot to handle. Rather, they slow the conversation down so that they can listen to the varied perspectives being expressed. Members with controversial views are not blocked or ignored; rather, members work hard to hear and understand.

As we develop our communications patience abilities, we develop the spirit of inquiry that promotes team learning. When feeling disagreement, we explore the assumptions underlying all views to develop a deeper understanding. As each of us reflects on and shares our underlying assumptions, we learn that others see the situation in a different way. We begin to see the world not only from our narrow point of view but also from the perspectives of others. Each person adds to the common database—a collection of ideas that make the whole group smarter about what is and what could be.

Team designers and facilitators have an important role to play in establishing a climate to encourage communications patience. First and foremost, facilitators can design their meetings for real input by asking big questions that get to the heart of the matter and then providing ample time and opportunity for each member to share from his or her unique perspective. And so, what are the critical conversations that people need to have to move forward together? What questions will you pose so that people can have them? What data do you need to surface and explore together? Who can provide those data? What process will you use to have people move from exploration to evaluation to action?

TEAM FITNESS EXERCISES

To practice and build the listening skills for understanding, try the exercises Who's on First? (Exercise 3.9, page 159), Living in Another Person's World (Exercise 3.8, page 157), or Blind Square (Exercise 3.17, page 172).

Problem-Solving Skill #2: Synergy Skills

A cycling enthusiast who is a friend of ours shared a highlight of his cycling career. During a race, Phil was able to secure a spot in the pack, or the peloton, with the elite cyclists. Riding elbow-to-elbow with the pros at breakneck speed, Phil achieved and maintained a pace that he had never achieved before and could never have achieved while cycling alone. Phil, along with his fellow pack members, benefited from drafting. Drafting happens when riders are protected from the wind by the cyclists in front of them.

Taking turns at the front, all cyclists benefiting from drafting were able to set and maintain a speed that no one member could maintain on his or her own. This is *synergy*—all members together achieving an outcome that each member individually

> Synergy occurs when the team's combined output is greater than the sum of the individual inputs. Synergy creates an excess of resources.

could not achieve and thus satisfying the needs of all. This shift toward creating synergy occurs when team members begin to understand that as individuals they do not possess the full truth or knowledge; rather, each member has both something to offer and something to learn. Synergy requires that people approach problems and solutions in a way that allows members to build on ideas, examine problems from many sides, and combine knowledge from many functions and perspectives.

Achieving synergy often requires creativity and risk. In our cycling example, it took all of Phil's physical and mental resources to ride elbow-to-elbow at top speed with the pack. Similarly, work-team members may experience risk when sharing new ideas or suggesting ideas that violate an existing protocol or accepted norm of practice.

We've isolated three techniques that are very helpful to the process of achieving synergy:

1. Preparation—Using data, not hunches. Teams collect important data and explore assumptions.

2. Generating and building on ideas. Teams use processes to generate many ideas and build on those ideas to produce breakthrough thinking.

3. Evaluating ideas and solutions. Teams test, evaluate, and tinker with ideas to generate synergistic solutions.

Synergy Technique #1: Preparation—using data, not hunches

<u>Collecting Facts</u>

Teams need good data to make good decisions. In the absence of good data, members waste time in pointless debates over opinions, and the problem with opinions is that we all have different ones.

Collecting accurate information is essential during all phases of the problem-solving process. Early on, good information is critical for identifying the right problem and understanding the full scope of the problem from each stakeholder's perspective. Throughout the problem-solving process, good data are essential for exploring and assessing options for workability. In short, the more information teams collect about their problem and its potential solutions, the more likely they are to craft the right problem statement and devise a workable solution.

Just as important as the collection of the data is how the team actually uses the data. In fact, as Daniel Goleman and colleagues point out, data interpretation is a core skill. Once data are collected, the ability to analyze them to create a shared understanding of "what it means" is in and of itself in a creative act (Goleman, Kaufmann, & Ray, 1992).

A good role model for collecting relevant facts and using them effectively is your family physician. The next time you visit your doctor with a complaint, observe how she collects data about you using a trial-and-error method of asking many questions. Exploring first by asking open-ended questions and listening attentively to your answers, your doctor narrows the questioning until she zeros in on a specific diagnosis. The physician then tests her assumptions by collecting more data. She may order tests or prescribe a medication. If the medication works, your problem is solved. If not, the process begins again until the correct diagnosis is made.

A team's information should come from many sources. What do the records say? Do we have the relevant statistics, and if not, how can we collect them? What are the opinions, wants, and needs of important stakeholders such as customers and suppliers? What do the experts say about important trends concerning the problem? What are your competitors doing? Who has solved this problem before? What did they learn? What other disciplines have tackled this problem before? How might we adapt their solutions?

Exploring Assumptions

We all hold taken-for-granted assumptions about the way things are or the way they should be. We don't question these assumptions or even think about them, but we hold them to be *true* for ourselves as well as others. "Children should be seen and not heard," "Managers decide, employees do," "Work is from 9:00 A.M.–5:00 P.M." are just a few examples.

Of course, the assumptions that I hold may be very different from the assumptions that you hold. When team members hold on tightly to their assumptions and do not discuss or question them, the stage is set for friction and conflict. We ask team members not to throw away their assumptions, but to practice "putting them aside" to help facilitate listening and understanding. Exploring assumptions raises the quality of thinking and sharing as it permits members to share the *whys* behind their views. With this deeper look, members can clearly distinguish between facts (i.e., objective reality) and perception (i.e., a subjective interpretation of reality formed from our assumptions).

Once assumptions have been surfaced, team members have important information that they can build on. The challenge is to help members clarify their assumptions, discover contradictions in their assumptions, if there are any, and then think through new strategies based on more-accurate assumptions. Bringing key assumptions to the surface can greatly increase creativity, as assumptions left unexamined limit the range of possible actions to the familiar and comfortable.

Checklist: Exploring Assumptions

To explore assumptions, ask open-ended questions to develop a deep understanding of the speaker's thoughts, feelings, and beliefs. Keep this checklist of questions available to use as needed to help surface assumptions and aid understanding.

Ask members to explore their assumptions of reality.

❖ What information are you basing that on? What evidence do you have? What facts do you have to confirm that?
❖ What are the assumptions that must be true in order for this solution to work?

Ask members to share how they interpret a scenario.

❖ If we do x, is y likely to occur? What are all the assumptions that must be true for y to occur?

Test assumptions held by the group.

❖ What assumptions are evident in the decisions we have made so far?
❖ Are they still valid? How have they changed?
❖ How have these assumptions limited us?

Ask members to share the reasons *why* they feel the way they do.

❖ What's your opinion of x?
❖ Do you think it will work? Why or why not?
❖ How do you think people will react if we do x? Why?
❖ What are your concerns?

Ask members to share what's important to them.

❖ If our plan were a huge success, what outcomes would we achieve?
❖ Why is this solution important to you?
❖ What criteria must we meet to achieve a solution that we can all live with?

Team Fitness Exercises

To help your team explore assumptions, refer to the following exercises: Concept Challenge (Exercise 3.10, page 160) and/or Exploring Assumptions (Exercise 3.14, page 165).

Synergy Technique #2: Generating and building on ideas

Creative problem solving requires an outlook that allows team members to search for ideas, protect those ideas while they simmer, and then build on those ideas. Instead of jumping to a solution prematurely—with only one or two ideas from which to choose—creative problem solvers give themselves the space to generate many ideas because they know that the best ideas come when their creative juices are flowing. With a wide variety of ideas from which to choose, it's much easier to make good decisions.

In his well-known work, Dr. Edward De Bono divides thinking into two categories. One he terms *vertical thinking*, or the process of applying linear thought and logic to the situation. We use our vertical thinking when we strategize, evaluate, and action-plan. The other type of thinking he calls *lateral thinking*, which involves disrupting an apparent thought sequence and arriving at a solution from another angle. Lateral thinking leads to those ideas that are simple only after they have been thought of. Indeed, as eminent business philosopher Peter Drucker points out, "The greatest praise an innovator can receive is for people to say 'This is so obvious. Why didn't I think of it?'"

Friends of ours in the improvisation business play a game called "find another answer." In this game, participants are tasked with answering a silly question as quickly as possible. After providing the first answer, participants are then asked to provide a second answer within a matter of seconds. The game teaches people to search for multiple answers, and time and time again, they surprise themselves with the wit, humor, and creativity of their second answers.

However, because the ability to think imaginatively has often not been nourished in youth or adulthood, many of us do not naturally default to thinking creatively. Instead of fostering and building on new ideas by focusing on what might work, we tear ideas apart, focusing on what we assume cannot work. In our fast-paced and hectic work settings, we tend to over-rely on vertical thinking to make quick judgments that serve to confirm the status quo.

Hence, while most organizational leaders believe in the value of new and creative ideas, they often unknowingly squash the possibility for creative thought. They do this by taking away the factors that are necessary for supporting it, including time, flexibility, and the freedom to experiment. Those who have been tasked with solving an important problem with an unreasonable deadline, too few people, and lack of authority to try something new will understand just how binding these constraints are.

In addition to the external constraints limiting creative thought are those within us. Roger von Oech (1998) identified the attitudes on the right, which he refers to as *mental locks* because they lock our thinking in the same old vertical way. While these attitudes are necessary for most of what we do (who wants creative thinking at a stop sign?), they prevent us from thinking flexibly when we are trying to be creative.

These mental locks limit thinking, because what people don't notice, they can't see. The quotes below, although humorous today, show how limiting a reliance on vertical thinking can be.

Mental Locks: How to Clamp Down on Creative Thinking

* The Right Answer
* That's Not Logical
* Follow the Rules
* Be Practical
* Avoid Ambiguity
* To Err Is Wrong
* Play Is Frivolous
* That's Not My Area
* Don't Be Foolish
* I'm Not Creative

We would never suggest that lateral thinking should be used at the expense of logic. Rather, both thinking processes are useful and necessary to create truly synergistic results. While there is an important place for critical evaluation and judgment, there is also a place for imaginative thinking that gives members the space to explore and innovate first. As you can see, critical judgment at the expense of imagination destroys opportunity.

"What use could the company make of an electric toy?"
Western Union, turning down the rights to the telephone, 1878

"Who the hell wants to hear actors talk?"
Harry Warner, President of Warner Bros. Pictures, 1922

"Everything that can be invented has been invented."
Charles Duell, Commissioner, U.S. Patents Office, 1899

"The horse is here to stay, but the automobile is only a novelty, a fad."
President of the Michigan Savings Bank advising Henry Ford's lawyer not to invest in the Ford Motor Company.

"Heavier than air flying machines are impossible."
Lord Kelvin, 1895

SOURCE: Goleman et al. (1992)

In our search of the literature, we have found that systematic innovators apply some of the following techniques.

Generate Promising Ideas

The first step is to cast a wide web to capture good ideas. Innovative teams are always on the alert for interesting ideas. They study markets, businesses, and industries that are the same as and different from their own to examine just what works and why. They see old ideas as the primary fodder for new ones.

Norm for Creativity

Just as important as each member's attitude toward innovation is the team's ability to foster a climate that accepts new ideas and agrees to control any knee-jerk negativity that may accompany new and "wacky" ideas. These teams nurture the creative spirit in members and protect partial ideas so that they can be adapted and built upon. Naïve questions are encouraged because they help members break out of their linear thought patterns and question assumptions that may no longer be valid.

So instead of imagining all the reasons why an idea can't work, the team allows the idea to develop fully and uses processes to imagine how an idea can work. With the voices of criticism stilled, members trust that they can express wild thoughts and propose imaginative ideas without having to invest all their energy in defending them.

Use Old Ideas in New Ways

Creative thinkers have the capacity to systematically use old ideas in new ways, new places, and new combinations. For example, the steam engine was used in mines for 75 years before Robert Fulton applied it to boats to create the first commercial steamboat. Similarly, Ford's first car, the Model T, looked strikingly similar to a horse-drawn carriage. He simply (or not so simply) replaced the real horsepower with the engine.

Consider how a team from 3M focused on creating a breakthrough product for the division's surgical drapes unit. While their initial goal was to create a better type of surgical draping, after observing surgeons in developing countries they revised their goal as simply *producing low-cost methods for infection control.*

With this new insight, the team set out to find leaders in the field from whom they could learn. Some of their most valuable learning came from experts in surprising places. For example, they found that their problem was similar to one that had been resolved by veterinarians whose patients are covered with hair, don't bathe, and don't have medical insurance. Another source was Hollywood. Makeup artists are experts in applying materials to the skin that are easy to put on and take off and that do not irritate the skin. These insights and others inspired the team to generate three strong proposals, with one breakthrough product—an antimicrobial protection cream to coat catheters and tubes aimed at controlling airborne diseases (Hargadon & Sutton, 2000).

TEAM FITNESS EXERCISES

The series of exercises beginning on page 72 will help a team develop an inquisitive mind. Experiment with them when the team is stuck in linear thinking: We guarantee they'll be fun and profitable.

Synergy Technique #3: Evaluating ideas and solutions
Innovative problem-solving teams tinker. Instead of endless debating about whether an idea will work or not, they collect data or, better yet, turn their idea into a product or service that can be tested and adapted. Putting ideas and concepts to the test gives teams important feedback they can use to improve them, apply them in another way, or abandon them. By thinking through and responding to the various implications of ideas before we adopt them, promising solutions can be developed that members can commit to. In fact, teams that we have worked with tell us that they learn just as much from testing ideas that don't fly as testing those that do.

While evaluation is crucial, timing is also important. If evaluation of ideas is premature, good ideas are abandoned before they become great ideas. Although the role of a devil's advocate can be very helpful, we don't recommend it as a permanent one for any specific team member. We've all been on teams where one or two members take great pride in playing the role of naysayer, blocking ideas that they personally do not support in the name of devil's advocate. The result is often frustration and inaction, as the team is effectively blocked from making decisions.

So how do you achieve the critical role of evaluation? All ideas must finally be put through a rigorous testing and examination for flaws. At some point, members must be ready and willing to switch from idea generation to evaluation. We suggest that evaluation of ideas be undertaken as a team activity. This way, all members focus first on creating and building the ideas and then on evaluating those ideas for feasibility. You will see that we have built this process (first creation of ideas and then evaluation) into most of our exercises. For example, in the visioning process, first we generate ideal futures and then we have a reality dialogue to assess whether the ideas can actually be achieved.

Synergy-Building Exercises and Techniques
The following exercises are designed to help members expand their thinking—that is, to discover aspects of an issue that they had not thought of or considered before—and/or to evaluate ideas for plausibility. Some of

our favorites are built on the work of creativity experts Edward De Bono and Roger von Oech. Select and experiment with the techniques that suit your team culture best. Remember, for the techniques to work, the team leader or facilitator must provide a safe, respectful environment.

Commit these techniques to memory and use them often during the journey through problem-solving sessions.

To Generate and Build On Ideas

Brainstorm

Ask members to generate as many ideas or options as they can without censorship or judgment (refer to Exercise 3.12, Brainstorming, page 163).

Challenge a Concept

Choose a concept. Ask members the following questions:

- ❖ Why must we do it this way?
- ❖ What other alternatives may there be?

(Refer to Exercise 3.10, Concept Challenge, page 160.)

Examine All Perspectives

Ask members to consider the following:

- ❖ Who is affected?
- ❖ How are they impacted?
- ❖ What are their needs?

Remove All Fault

Ask members to assume no fault or blame.

Change Your Viewpoint

Ask members to think about and consider the viewpoints of others.

Ask a Different Question

When members have exhausted their ideas for one question, ask the question in a different way. For example, after asking, "Where will we go on our holidays?" you may also ask, "What do we want to do on our holidays?" Different questions spark different answers.

Ask Your Questions in Plural

Simply frame your questions in a way that generates more than one right answer. Instead of asking, "What's the answer?" ask, "What are the answers?"

<u>To Evaluate Ideas</u>

Consider All Factors

Ask members to search for all the factors involved in a situation. To practice, refer to Exercise 3.11, Consider All Factors, on page 161.

Pluses, Minuses, So What?

Ask members to identify all the pluses and minuses of a particular scenario or option. On the basis of their data, ask them to explore "so what?" or how we can adapt our decision to accommodate the pluses and minimize the minuses. To practice, see Exercise 3.16, Pluses, Minuses, So What? on page 171.

Consequences and Sequels

Ask members to identify all the probable consequences of a particular scenario in the short term, the medium term, and the longer term. On the basis of the data you generate, ask members to adopt, modify, or abandon their idea. To practice, refer to Exercise 3.15, Consequences and Sequels, on page 169.

Evaluation Matrix

Ask members to identify important criteria for assessing the feasibility of several ideas. Criteria may include factors such as cost, ease of implementation, value to customer, and impact. Each criterion can be weighted to reflect its relative importance. For each idea, participants then assess whether the idea meets the criteria by answering yes, no, or maybe.

Problem-Solving Skill #3:
Using a Disciplined Problem-Solving Process

There are many structured problem-solving processes available, and it is very likely that your organization has adopted one. This is good, and if your team is using it, even better. However, even though we know we should follow a disciplined sequence of problem-solving steps, we have a great temptation to skip a few and arrive at a decision prematurely.

The tremendous value of a problem-solving process is that it helps to align our thinking and action around a common approach to the following actions:

- ❖ Selecting the problem
- ❖ Exploring the problem and gathering data
- ❖ Establishing success criteria
- ❖ Developing a clear problem statement

❖ Generating options

❖ Evaluating options

❖ Selecting a preferred solution

❖ Developing a plan for team action

❖ Testing and modifying the solution

Nine Steps: Tips and techniques for winning team problem-solving

Our version of the problem-solving process incorporates many of the techniques we have discussed so far. Use it and adapt it to suit your team's needs.

Step 1: Select the Problem

To select a problem, follow these steps:

❖ Begin with team's mission and vision.

❖ Identify the gaps between desired future state and current reality.

❖ List all barriers to achieving future state; these are your problems.

❖ Collect data from customers and stakeholders.

❖ Choose problem using relevant criteria (payoff, speed, "bee in the bonnet" issue, etc.).

Step 2: Explore the Problem

Assess possible causes and interpretations of the problem:

❖ Collect the facts.

❖ Examine all sides.

❖ Define stakeholder interests.

❖ Surface assumptions.

Step 3: Establish Success Criteria

Set objective standards for evaluating possible solutions:

❖ Review the stakeholder interests that must be met.

❖ Identify the boundaries that must be respected (e.g., legislation, time frames, policies).

❖ Challenge all boundaries to reduce blocks to creativity.

❖ Connect the success criteria back to the mission and vision.

Step 4: Develop a Problem-Solving Statement or Goal

❖ Write a problem or goal statement that all members are committed to solving.

* Review and gain agreement on the expectations of the team to decide, recommend, or simply generate options.
* Gain agreement on the method of decision making: vote, consensus, unanimity, and so on.

Step 5: Generate Many Options

Expand the thinking to create many options:

* Brainstorm.
* Dialogue.
* Combine ideas.
* Do not evaluate.

Step 6: Assess Options

Evaluate options against the previously established success criteria:

* Ask which options best meet our needs.
* Develop a matrix of options and criteria and rank each option.
* Eliminate options with flaws.

Step 7: Select Preferred Solution

* Identify and select the option(s) that best meet success criteria.
* Consider the consequences of preferred options.
* Consider the pluses, minuses, and *so what?*s of each option.
* Ask how options can be combined or modified to create superior solutions.
* Review the agreed-upon solution and test for consensus.

Step 8: Develop an Action Plan

* Create goals and action plans specifying individual and team accountabilities.

Step 9: Test and Modify

Evaluate the success of your efforts:

* Assess metrics to determine if the solution is achieving the intended goal.
* Assess whether stakeholders are pleased with the solution.
* Modify plans to accommodate ongoing interests, data, and events.

Communications Patience, Synergy, and Process Skills: The Proven Formula to Create Problem-Solving Team Pros

The skills of patient communications and building synergy may seem simple to understand, but they are not simple to carry out. They require a different orientation, whereby team members slow down to share important information and perspectives and also take their time to explore the gifts, talents, and perspectives of their fellow team members. To develop these skills, begin by watching your own communication style and the communication patterns in your team. Are team members working together by leveraging the ideas of all, or are members prematurely abandoning ideas, leaving them to dissipate into thin air? If so, the resultant conflict and misunderstanding may be occurring because team members are not taking the time and energy to share, listen, build on ideas, and evaluate them before springing to action.

This realization—that team conflict and friction arise because of differing working styles, diverse perspectives, and the inherent noise in the communication process and not because of the inadequacies of the members—is a crucial first step. With this realization comes a step toward respect and genuine liking for fellow team members. It takes the negative energy away from relationship issues and more appropriately focuses the energy where it belongs—on dialoguing around the issues and problems to be solved.

Handling Team Conflict 4

Handling Team Conflict: Signpost #3 of Team Success

The third vital sign for healthy teams is the ability to handle team conflict. Conflict among team members is an inevitable part of group life. People pulled together to work on complex issues will naturally experience frictions associated with diverse working styles, thinking styles, behavioral norms, and performance expectations. Our research, supported by others (for example, Moore, 1986), indicates that it's how people work with the conflict that determines whether the conflict is a positive and productive force or a destructive force. And so, if we can offer one piece of advice for handling team conflict, it is this: "Do not avoid it." Avoiding conflict not only stifles creativity, it creates barriers to relationships that can ultimately pull the team apart. Rather than avoiding it, we suggest that team members develop an orientation to conflict that allows them to expect it, work through it, and learn and grow from it.

Our research has found that teams that have established sound team management practices and problem-solving skills have fewer conflicts. This makes sense intuitively, because establishing team management practices forces team members to identify behavioral norms and to develop a common understanding of their purpose, objectives, and strategies. This alone removes many potential sources of team friction. Furthermore, teams with well-developed problem-solving abilities have developed the capacity to seek out and build on diverse views rather than stifle them. Even with well-developed team management practices and problem-solving skills, most teams from time to time will encounter issues that can lead to friction and interpersonal strain. This chapter will help your team anticipate potential conflicts and work through them as they happen.

> ### Research Note: Some Friction Actually Boosts Creativity
>
> As previously discussed, not all conflict is bad; in fact, some conflict is good. Our research, supported by that of others (including Janis, 1972; Hall & Watson, 1970; and Deutsch, 1969), shows that teams that encourage diverse views and have processes to harness creative friction are better problem solvers and report higher levels of team performance and satisfaction than teams that avoid it.

Conflict can be defined as either substantive conflict—when members have differences of opinion about what the facts mean, about what should be done, or about how the team should implement a decision—or affective conflict—when members personalize differences of opinion, style, or personality, characterizing other members as "lazy," "stupid," or "untrustworthy." While a healthy respect for substantive conflict allows members to stay on task and work through tough issues to enhance team learning and creativity, affective conflict siphons the team's energy from the work at hand and produces counterproductive actions such as squabbling and turf protection. Too much affective, or personalized, conflict is detrimental to teams (Bell & Blakeney, 1977) and negatively impacts both performance and satisfaction (Wall, Galanes, & Love, 1987). Often, affective conflict takes hold insidiously, when members breach behavioral norms that others hold dear, perhaps by arriving late or not completing team tasks on time. Even if these norms have not been articulated, some members fume in silence, believing that "any normal person" would know better.

Having skills and processes in place to deal with team conflict can deflect these crises and help the team turn potentially negative conflicts into opportunities for learning and growth.

Tools for Handling Team Conflict

The tools described in the following pages are designed to promote understanding of team conflict, focusing on the following two key areas:

Diagnosing the key causes of conflict—Analyzing the causes of conflict so that it can be managed appropriately

Conflict styles and protocols for managing conflicts—Understanding how the team deals with diversity and disruptive behaviors as they occur

DIAGNOSING THE KEY CAUSES OF CONFLICT

Every year, we benefit from the wisdom and expertise of conflict management gurus Chris Moore and Judy Mares Dixon of CDR Associates when they visit Queen's University to teach mediation skills.

One of their key insights is that the root causes of conflict must be understood before an appropriate intervention strategy can be created. Chris Moore's Circle of Conflict (Figure 4.1) provides a useful tool for diagnosing the causes of conflict.

What Causes Conflict or a Dispute?

The **Circle of Conflict** outlines some of the major sources of conflict, regardless of level (interpersonal, intraorganizational or interorganizational, communal, or societal) or setting. The circle identifies five central causes of conflict:

- ❖ Problems with people's relationships
- ❖ Problems with data
- ❖ Perceived or actual incompatible interests
- ❖ Structural forces
- ❖ Differing values

Relationship conflicts occur because of the presence of strong negative emotions, misperceptions or stereotypes, poor or miscommunication, or repetitive negative behaviors. These problems often result in what has been called unrealistic (Coser, 1956) or unnecessary (Moore, 1986) conflicts since they may occur even when objective conditions for a conflict, such as limited resources or mutually exclusive goals, are not present. Relationship problems, such as those previously listed, often fuel disputes and lead to an unnecessary escalating spiral of destructive conflict.

Data conflicts occur when people lack information necessary to make wise decisions, are misinformed, disagree over what data are relevant, interpret information differently, or have competing assessment procedures. Some data conflict may be unnecessary since it is caused by poor communication

---

(Continued)

(Continued)

between the people in conflict. Other data conflicts may be genuine because the information and/or procedures used by the people to collect data are not compatible.

Interest conflicts are caused by competition over perceived or actual incompatible needs. Conflicts of interest result when one or more parties believe that in order to satisfy his or her needs, those of an opponent must be sacrificed. Interest-based conflicts occur over substantive issues (money, physical resources, time, etc.), procedural issues (the way the dispute is to be resolved), or psychological issues (perceptions of trust, fairness, desire for participation, respect, etc.). For an interest-based dispute to be resolved, all parties must have a significant number of their interests addressed and/or met in each of these three areas.

The **Satisfaction Triangle** illustrates the interdependence of these three kinds of needs. The triangle, or a settlement, is not complete unless there is satisfaction on each of the three sides. A satisfactory substantive settlement without procedural and psychological satisfaction may be inadequate to induce a final agreement.

Conflicts often result when one or more of the people in conflict adopt a position that allows only one solution to meet their needs. Generally interests can be satisfied in a variety of ways (Fisher & Ury, 1983).

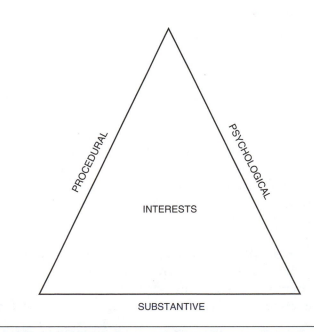

Figure 4.1   Satisfaction Triangle

Copyright 1996 CDR Associates

Structural conflicts are caused by oppressive patterns of human relationships (Galtung, 1975). These patterns are often shaped by forces external to the people in dispute. Limited physical resources or authority, geographic constraints (distance or proximity), time (too little or too much), organizational structures, and so forth, often promote conflict behavior.

Value conflicts are caused by perceived or actual incompatible belief systems. Values are beliefs that people use to give meaning to their lives. Values explain what is good or bad, right or wrong, just or unjust. Differing values need not cause conflict. People can live together in harmony with quite different value systems. Value disputes arise only when people attempt to force one set of values on others or lay claims to exclusive value systems which do not allow for divergent beliefs.

The Circle of Conflict and Conflict Mapping

The Circle of Conflict is a useful analytical tool for examining disputes and uncovering the root cause of conflict behavior. By examining a conflict and evaluating it

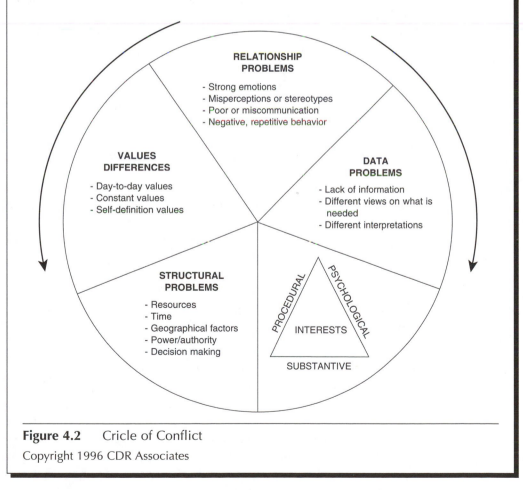

Figure 4.2   Cricle of Conflict

Copyright 1996 CDR Associates

(Continued)

(Continued)

according to the five categories—relationship, data, interest, structure, and value—we can begin to determine what causes the dispute, identify what sector is primary, and assess whether the cause is a genuine incompatibility of interests or perceptual problems of involved parties. These insights can assist us in designing a resolution strategy that will have a higher probability of success than an approach which is exclusively trial and error (Moore, 1986).

Cooperating Versus Competing

A useful exercise for helping team members understand the many causes of conflict is Win All You Can on page 177. In this exercise, the participants are divided into four teams and are presented with a forced-choice decision to either cooperate by showing a Y card or compete by showing an X card. The reward strategy is set up so that if one team competes and the others do not, the competing team wins three points and the cooperating teams lose a point. If all teams cooperate, they all win one point. Teams have 2 minutes to make a decision for each round, and most games include 8–10 rounds.

What's critical here is that, on the surface, the competing strategy appears to be the choice that will afford teams the most points, and over the course of the game, most teams naturally fall into competition. In actuality, teams who compete rarely, if ever, win. Let's explore the rules of the game with Chris Moore's Circle of Conflict to see why.

Problems with data—The game is laden with sources of data conflict. The instructions are intentionally fuzzy, team members are not given sufficient time to review them with each other or the instructor, and time pressures force members to begin the game and make a decision before all members understand the payoff structure. With no opportunity to create joint goals and build trust before the first round of decision making, typically at least one team opts to compete, thereby setting the scene for win-lose competition.

Perceived or actual incompatible interests—There is great confusion around the game's ultimate purpose. Are the teams supposed to maximize their own score or the joint scores of all teams? With no opportunity for the teams to talk to each other to clarify the ultimate purpose and establish joint interests, they typically fall into competition. Later in the game, when a spokesperson from each team is permitted to meet in the hall to plan for the next round, teams find it difficult to build support for a cooperative strategy unless they are able to rebuild trust.

Structural forces—Many sources of structural conflict exist. The teams are separated to create geographical and social boundaries, and they are not permitted to communicate with each other. Lack of communication seriously inhibits trust. Intrateam conflicts surface as members are forced to make a group decision with insufficient information and processing time. The intrateam dynamics are made more complex with the introduction of a cross-functional group of spokespeople who in later rounds are permitted to meet and plan in the hall before returning to their home team for final decision making.

Value differences—Value conflicts occur when one group tries to impose its value system on another. Typically, two value systems emerge over the course of the game. Those teams who strongly adhere to the values associated with cooperation tend to make the decision to cooperate for all rounds, independent of the actions of the other groups. While these teams see themselves as "doing the right thing," they are often labeled as naïve by the others. On the other hand, some teams make a decision to compete at all costs, even if they have communicated to the other teams that they will cooperate. These teams, with a strong value for winning and competition, are typically labeled by the others as untrustworthy.

Relationship issues—Even though there are no relationship issues (the X and the Y have no real meaning, except for the points they confer), people create relationship issues by assigning attributes to the offenders who compete.

The debriefing can be a real eye-opener for team members as they make these important discoveries:

❖ It is normal and natural for members to experience conflict. Often conflict is a result of the situation that members find themselves in and not a result of interpersonal differences.

❖ People often assign personal causes to a conflict that is actually caused by a structural or data-related or interest-based issue. This causes unnecessary strain on team relationships.

   ❖ When conflict is personalized, people fall into the "blame frame" and abandon responsibility for proactively trying to solve the problem.

   ❖ Relationships and trust are built through acts of kindness, support, and keeping our promises. Trust is broken instantly when someone breaks a promise or even acts in a way that is perceived by others to be unsupportive.

Open, two-way, and preferably face-to-face communication between people and groups is a critical ingredient in preventing interpersonal conflicts. When people have the opportunity to clarify joint aims, the facts, their assumptions, and the alternatives, they can stay focused on the task and can move forward. Hence, teams in data conflict will become productive again if they invest time and energy in defining their data requirements, getting the data they need, and analyzing the data. Teams experiencing structural conflict may need to adjust their pace if time pressures are prohibitive, meet more often if geography is an issue, or redefine their approach if the process is not working for them. The critical lesson is that if the causes of conflict are inappropriately attributed to relationship or interpersonal differences, they will continue to occur and eventually block the group from doing its work.

TEAM FITNESS EXERCISE

A useful exercise for helping members understand the many causes of conflict is Exercise 4.1, Win All You Can (see page 177).

CONFLICT STYLES AND PROTOCOLS FOR MANAGING CONFLICT

It's Friday afternoon at 3:15, and your team meeting was supposed to start at 3:00. Everyone is present, except for Brenda, who is late again. The team has agreed that being on time for meetings is an important norm. At 3:25 P.M., she rushes in, apologizing for her tardiness and explaining that the computer ate her document.

Which of the following are members most likely to do?

1. Ignore the problem and continue discussion

2. Acknowledge the problem but do nothing to correct the situation

3. Acknowledge the problem and attempt to solve it

4. Acknowledge the problem, solve it, and discuss and agree on a procedure for dealing with similar problems in the future

An important determinant of how members respond to conflict is their conflict-handling style. While each member of the team has a natural style for handling conflict (Thomas, 1976), team members can learn to adapt their style to fit various situations, and teams can create norms and protocols to guide how they approach conflict. The preferred conflict-handling styles of team members, and teams as well, fall into four pure categories (Thomas, 1976):

❖ **Avoiding.** Members choose not to confront or be involved. In the previous case, members would choose to ignore Brenda's tardiness, even though they are bothered by it.

❖ **Accommodating.** Members adapt or agree to satisfy the needs of others above their own needs. Here, members might choose to sympathize with Brenda and not raise the issue. As a result, Brenda will probably be late for the next meeting as well.

❖ **Competing.** Members choose to satisfy their own needs by asserting, controlling, or resisting. Here, members would likely confront Brenda by telling her in no uncertain terms that her tardiness is unacceptable and dictate their expectations for the future: Be on time, or else.

❖ **Collaborating.** Members attempt to create mutually satisfying solutions through win-win strategies. Here, members would likely acknowledge the problem, explore the causes, and work with Brenda to create a protocol that will meet the team's needs and Brenda's as well.

Not surprisingly, teams in our study who took an approach of openly acknowledging the problem and working collaboratively to put in place a procedure for dealing with similar occurrences in the future reported higher levels of team satisfaction and performance.

Of course, teams that create a healthy environment for conflict handling are not immune to problems. From time to time, members will inadvertently annoy others by violating team norms for punctuality, participation, or active listening. However, in skilled teams, members do not ignore or smooth over these felt infractions. Rather, members bring them to the surface right away by focusing on the behavior to be changed, while at the same time ensuring they don't attack or belittle the perpetrator.

Take Sue, for example, who as a last-minute consideration invited her colleague Tom to a meeting she had arranged with a client. During the meeting, Tom and the client got along famously, while Sue felt ignored. Following the meeting, Sue did not walk away demonizing Tom as an insensitive clod who did not value or respect her. Rather, Sue met with Tom and explained how she felt. Tom was aghast. It turned out that Tom was not even aware that Sue felt left out, and he was truly sorry. They then talked about how they would prevent a similar occurrence in the future. This proactive response to a conflict situation repaired the relationship fully.

In contrast, team members who do not raise and work through differences or "felt injustices" as they occur will find that the issues collect and fester over time and tend to explode into crises at the most inconvenient times—when deadlines loom and stress is high, for example. At worst, team members use either passive avoidance (nonparticipation) or aggressive behavior (stubbornness, perfectionism, and loud talk) in dealing with each other. Years of conflict build layers of mistrust that must be addressed and healed.

And so, once again, our advice to teams is do not avoid conflict. Rather, as irritants occur, put in place respectful processes to acknowledge the issue, resolve it, and discuss and agree on a procedure for dealing with similar problems in the future. Using this approach, members don't view conflict as one-sided, whereby one member is doing something to another. This kind of thinking is reactive and leads to blaming—a dangerous poison for teams. When we go into a blaming mode, we view ourselves as "right or good or true" and begin to demonize the other as "wrong or uncaring or disrespectful." In the blame frame, we move into reactivity and abandon our responsibility for doing our part to find a workable solution. We do not listen, we do not challenge our assumptions, and we do not ask questions to understand. We simply abdicate our responsibility and expect others to fix themselves.

Team Fitness Exercise

Exercise 4.2, Handling Problems in Team Discussion Assessment on page 182, is a useful tool for assessing how the team handles disruptions as they occur.

After completing this exercise, the team can have a rich and meaningful discussion on the norms and behaviors it would like to reinforce for healthy team conflict handling. Despite these interventions, sometimes members experience serious difficulty with each other. Deeply felt personality conflicts can undermine the team's efforts unless they are dealt with openly and directly. In this situation, we encourage the team leader to hold a private meeting with the individuals involved and to clearly address the behavior changes needed. Sometimes, despite all efforts, there will be rare occasions when a team member will have to be replaced. Our research has identified that some people have a strong preference for working independently and may not be able to adapt to a collective work environment.

Fostering a Supportive Infrastructure for Teams 5

The Big Question: Are You Really Ready for Teams?

In today's turbulent corporate environments, thriving organizations are turning to teams to respond to the complexity of the business world.

Forces for responsiveness, speed, and service are driving decision making to all levels of the organization, where the information, expertise, and experience can be gathered more quickly and easily.

While more and more organizations are experimenting with team-based structures, we caution leaders to take a thoughtful approach to implementing them. Implementing teams is hard work and requires a major rethinking of management systems, behaviors, and attitudes. If a team-based structure is implemented without careful planning, the leadership may simply be replacing one problematic structure with another.

If you are wondering whether moving to a team-based structure is right for your organization, carefully consider your answers to the following questions. If most answers support the need for teams, your organization is probably ripe for team implementation. If you are not sure, study your organization to identify where and how teams may be helpful.

FIFTEEN QUESTIONS: ARE TEAMS THE ANSWER FOR YOUR ORGANIZATION?

1. Does your organization need to coordinate parts of the work that have so far been done in separate units to increase speed, quality, or innovation?

2. Is there a need to strengthen linkages between groups and units?

3. Does your organization face moderate to high uncertainty in its environment (complex and changing fast)?

4. Has decision making been slow or poor up to this point?

5. Has there been too much conflict among units up to this point?

6. Has knowledge sharing between groups and units been poor up to this point?

7. Is there a need for increasing responsibility and accountability at the work unit level?

8. Do organization members feel a strong need for the team-based structure? Do they also feel a sense of urgency to get on with the transition?

9. Are your top managers committed to working as a real team?

10. Does the organization have a clear understanding of the key functions teams would be responsible for and the key linkages required for coordination?

11. Do leaders and managers have a common mindset that favors employee participation and empowerment?

12. Does the organization have a plan for transferring authority to the teams?

13. Do managers and supervisors have a clear understanding about how their roles will change with the new team structure?

14. Do they have the capability to fulfill these new roles?

15. Will your organization commit to training team members and supervisors in their new roles?

The Art and Science of Implementing Teams

"Where did we go wrong?" exclaimed a well-intentioned yet frustrated manager of a large manufacturing facility. "We asked employees to come up with ideas for teams, but only a few teams have formed. We want the ideas for teams to come from them, not us." And so the story goes of senior managers committed to the idea of teams but unaware of their role in managing the transition and creating a supportive infrastructure for teams to develop and flourish.

Unfortunately this scenario is a common one. As a result, the whole notion of teams has fallen out of favor with many management groups. Teams that are left unsupported often peter out and disband. It is the rare team that can create the necessary structures, systems, and relationships to succeed without the support and help of their leadership.

For most employees, line and staff alike, adjusting to a team-based structure requires a fundamental change in the way they work. While managers must learn to coach and facilitate, their employees must accept greater responsibility and learn new skills.

In moving to a team-based structure, the leadership's role is a critical one. Not only must they create the infrastructure to support and reinforce the new work methods, relationships, and reporting requirements, they must also be actively involved in leading the transition to the new work environment. In short, moving to a team-based structure is a major change initiative that requires thoughtful planning and role modeling from the top team. If the leadership does not provide this critical direction and support, employees will remain rooted in old patterns of working, as shown in the example of the frustrated plant manager.

We will now examine the change-management literature in relation to implementing teams. Use it as a guide to the process of introducing and supporting teams in your organization.

Research Roundup: Applying Change
Management Theory to Team Implementation

Change-management theory can help us understand why teams require the strong support of management as they adapt to the new work environment. In all change efforts, small or systemwide, there are three phases (Beckhard 1969):

- ❖ The present, or the way things are
- ❖ The future, or the way things will be
- ❖ The transition, the phase during which the change takes place

Richard Beckhard and Wendy Pritchard (1992) liken this transition to shifting gears in your automobile; you can't move from one gear to another without first going through neutral. Similarly, for any change, a transition state—a state in which employees must first shed old behaviors and attitudes—is needed before they can adopt new behaviors and attitudes.

A colleague of ours, Deborah Mackin, refers to this transition state as the *muck in the middle.* The muck occurs when we begin to take action and learn firsthand that the road is steep and bumpy in places and wet and boggy in others. As we hit the bumps, we feel unsettled, unsure, unproductive, and frustrated. What once worked no longer works and new systems have yet to be created. Our feet are firmly planted in the muck when we forget the vision, when the decisions get tough, when roles and structures get confusing, and when the pain starts to be felt. Trials and tribulations along the way cause people to doubt the vision, doubt the leadership, and even doubt themselves. People become nostalgic for yesterday, even when the past was far from ideal.

Understanding the transition process is critical to helping people accept change. In the following section, we offer several foundational theories of change and provide a blueprint for leading people through the transition process.

Kurt Lewin's Unfreezing, Moving, and Refreezing

While working with the anthropologist Margaret Mead during World War II, Kurt Lewin conducted the first of many experiments that led him to define change as a three-phase process: "unfreezing, moving, and refreezing" (Lewin, 1953). *Unfreezing* is the process of creating change readiness; through a joint discovery of what is or what could be, people learn why change is necessary. *Moving* is the process of changing; people implement the change goals and, through a process of experimenting and testing, adopt new behaviors, attitudes, and perceptions. In this phase, people plan, learn, and implement the change. *Refreezing* is the process of creating structures and norms to support the change to create the new norm. Here, people incorporate new processes and behaviors into their routines. Refer to "Building Support for Beef Hearts, Sweetbreads, and Kidneys" for a detailed description of Lewin's thought-provoking initial experiment.

Lewin's pioneering work and three-phase theory of change has set the foundation for most subsequent research and thinking about change management. It is commonly accepted that for a successful change to occur, leaders must develop a strategy for unfreezing the attitudes and behaviors of individuals and groups involved in the change. They then must develop strategies for introducing new behaviors and expectations before refreezing the new attitudes and behaviors to support the change state. All of this requires careful planning and expert implementation, as we shall see in the pages that follow.

Building Support for
Beef Hearts, Sweetbreads, and Kidneys

The setting was Iowa during World War II, when Lewin was asked to help reduce civilian consumption of rationed foods, mainly meat. The problem was that even though traditional meats were scarce, families were resistant to trying other nonscarce meats such as beef hearts, sweetbreads, and kidneys.

Knowing that housewives were the shoppers and preparers of food, Lewin reasoned that they were the gatekeepers who controlled the situation. He believed that if the housewives were given new information and allowed to participate in deciding what to do, they would be more likely to change their shopping habits and prepare meals with the nonscarce meats.

To test this hypothesis, Lewin set up a controlled experiment with several groups of housewives. In one group, a nutrition expert lectured the group on the facts as well as the benefits of cooking and consuming the nonscarce meats, emphasizing both the health and economic benefits. The expert offered preparation and cooking tips and handed out recipes of her family's favorite dishes.

In the other three groups, the women were given the facts and asked to discuss and create their own meal plans. The nutrition expert offered advice and recipes only after the group had decided that cooking the nonscarce meats had merit. You may well have guessed the outcome. Groups in the "discuss and decide ourselves" groups were more likely to actually change their eating habits than the groups who were lectured to. Specifically, while 3% of the group that was lectured to actually tried one of the nonscarce meats, 32% of the "discuss and decide ourselves" groups actually prepared the meats for their families.

Lewin believed that when people are involved in defining the change problem and designing the solution, they not only become aware of the need for change but also become committed to the action plans for implementing change. Simply put, they experience the process of unfreezing, moving, and refreezing, which empowers people to create change.

SOURCE: Lewin (1953)

(Continued)

(Continued)

Dannemiller's $D \times V \times F > R$

In the early 1980s, Kathie Dannemiller was asked by executives at the Ford Motor Company to train their managers to be "more participative" and to train them quickly. Ford, like many other North American automobile manufacturers, was losing market share to the Japanese automobile manufacturers. Ford executives believed that they needed to leverage the knowledge and talents of people working at every level and across all functions to regain a competitive position (Dannemiller Tyson Associates, 1994).

From the outside looking in, Dannemiller saw the Ford Motor Company as an *arthritic* organization, one in which narrowly defined policies, procedures, roles, and responsibilities prohibited people from adapting freely and flexibly to the new competition. Managers, each with their functional fiefdoms, were expert at telling and directing, not coaching and developing. In short, Dannemiller saw huge cultural resistance to the type of change the Ford executives proposed. She reasoned that simply training managers in participative management techniques would not transform their attitudes to thrive in a participative culture (Dannemiller Tyson Associates, 1994).

Building on the pivotal work of Beckhard (1969), who recognized that for change to occur, people must experience a greater pull toward the change than the pull they feel from the status quo, Dannemiller and her associates (1994) created a change process designed to energize a critical mass of stakeholders to accept and create change. Her change process is built on the notion that for change to occur, people must have a deep appreciation for the *why, what,* and *how* of the change, which they describe as follows:

> Our version states that for change to occur, the product of dissatisfaction with the present situation (D), a vision of what is possible (V), and first steps to reach the vision (F) must be greater than resistance to change (R).
>
> $$D \times V \times F > R$$
>
> If any element is missing, the product will be zero. Since we all resist change to some extent, if the product is zero we will not overcome resistance and no change will occur. In other words, if people are able to absorb new information, they will see the world differently (paradigm shift) and, once their paradigm shifts, their behaviour will change as a result. (Dannemiller Tyson Associates, 1994, p. 6)

Accordingly, Dannemiller created a series of workshops that brought together a critical mass of managers to discuss why their present situation was no longer viable (D), to create a clear vision of their preferred future (V), and to plan how they would get there (F). As these sessions began to produce fruitful results, they were cascaded to all other levels of the organization, creating support and momentum for the changes initiated at the top. The results of this initiative speak for themselves. At Ford, quality is job one.

Eight Steps to Implementing Teams: An Integrated Approach

While most managers are comfortable with strategic planning and creating visions, goals, and action plans, far fewer are aware of the need to actually manage the change process. Implementation of the change process, or managing the transition phase, is by far the most challenging task during change.

So what is management's role in creating a critical mass of employees who understand the need for teams, identify with the vision for the future, and are engaged in activities to make effective teams a reality?

We offer a number of complex and overlapping steps that must be managed in any major change effort (Beckhard & Harris, 1987; Dannemiller Tyson Associates, 1994; Kanter, Stein, & Jick, 1992; Kotter, 1996). These include the following:

1. Identify the change problem and direction.

2. Create the transition structure. Define who will guide the change.

3. Create a common understanding of why change is necessary.

4. Create and communicate a shared vision for success.

5. Develop an integrated change plan with strategies, tactics, and goals. Spread transformation efforts through the development and communication of tangible goals and objectives.

6. Align structures, processes, and resources to support the change.

7. Consolidate improvements and produce more change.

8. Integrate the change into the culture and institutionalize new approaches.

You will notice in the following chart that the steps of the change process follow the three-phase Lewin model of change by helping people unfreeze, move, and refreeze and well as educate people by creating a deep appreciation for the why, what, and how of change (see Figure 5.1). These steps, followed in the order presented here, provide a blueprint for

Planning	**Why**	**What**	**How**
1. Identify the change problem and direction	3. Create a common understanding of the need to change.	4. Create and communicate the vision for success.	5. Develop an integrated change plan with strategies, tactics, and goals.
2. Create the Transition Structure:	Be sure to identify and involve leaders, helpers, and other key power groups in a joint diagnosis for the need to change.	Involve key stakeholders so that they understand the overall change goals, the high-level strategy for reaching them, and their specific roles and responsibilities in moving forward.	6. Align structures, processes, and resources to enable participation.
Assign the individuals and teams who are charged with leading the initiative.			7. Consolidate improvements and produce more change.
Identify the key stakeholders (individuals and groups) who need to be involved and consulted along the way.			8. Integrate the change into the culture and institutionalize new approaches.

Figure 5.1   Eight Steps to Implementing Teams

successful change planning and implementation, including leadership's critical roles in each.

STEP #1: IDENTIFY THE CHANGE PROBLEM AND DIRECTION

All change initiatives should begin with a thorough diagnosis of the problem or opportunity that the organization wishes to address. Change leaders must survey their environment for important changes and then translate their diagnosis into strategies and structures that enable them to compete. As today's leaders focus on the critical task of designing an appropriate organizational structure to meet the challenges and opportunities they are facing, many are concluding that a flatter, team-based structure will promote a more efficient, agile, and customer-centric competitive response.

In considering a shift to a team-based structure, change leaders might begin by exploring how the current organizational form is supporting or blocking needed flexibility, agility, learning, and communications by asking the following questions:

❖ What are the forces compelling change in the external environment, be they political, economic, social, demographic, technological, and so forth?

- ❖ What are the implications of these changes for the way we do business?

- ❖ How might they alter our strategy, our structure, and our processes?

- ❖ What competencies do we need to develop?

- ❖ What organizational structure do we need to support the following:
  - The new work that needs to be done
  - The required integration among organizational departments or divisions
  - The required level of creativity, flexibility, and standardization
  - The required level of accountability and responsibility for decision making

- ❖ Will more teams or a team-based structure help us create the appropriate structural response?

STEP #2: CREATE THE TRANSITION STRUCTURE—DEFINE WHO WILL GUIDE THE CHANGE

By its very nature, change disrupts the business-as-usual operating environment. It therefore stands to reason that for meaningful change to be contemplated and new learning to occur, the people leading the change initiatives must be freed from the business-as-usual organizational hierarchy. Put simply, the work of change is unique, and a transition structure must be put in place to manage it (Beckhard & Harris, 1987; Kotter, 1996).

We recommend that a change sponsor and champion set up a steering team for change, or what John Kotter (1996) refers to as the guiding coalition. The responsibility of the change steering team is to identify all the activities that need to take place to prepare the organization for change, and then to manage the implementation. Thus, the

> ### Research Note: The Importance of Monomaniacs With a Mission
>
> In her research on implementing technological change in manufacturing facilities, Beatty (1987) found that change projects were more likely to be successful if a transition structure was in place to manage the change. The transition structure included a change sponsor (a senior leader who strongly supported the change and acted as a role model), a steering committee, and a change champion (a respected leader who was the principal organizer and driving force behind the change). Carol fondly refers to the change champion as a *monomaniac with a mission* (with credit to Peter Drucker). Visionary, persistent, skilled in communications, and patient yet firm, no barrier was allowed to block his or her path to achieving the change objective.

change team is responsible for creating a felt need for change, developing the vision, communicating the vision widely, empowering teams and individuals to take action, rewarding successes, and anchoring the new approaches in the organization's culture.

In that the steering team is responsible for planning and implementing the change, it must be composed of the right mix of people. Ideally, members should represent the interests and perspectives of the stakeholder groups most impacted by the change, whether they are union members, production employees, or sales staff. In addition, the team should include members who possess position power, expertise, credibility, leadership capability, and the ability to foster trust (Kotter, 1996).

A test that we often use in determining whether the steering team has the right membership is the *blockade test*. Simply put, the steering team has the right mix of members when it has enough key players that no persons left off the team are able to block the change from happening.

So, depending on the change, the steering team may include members who operate outside of the normal hierarchy such as union presidents, board members, internal experts, and rank-and-file employees, as well as senior and middle managers. While the initial steering team may be small, ideally it will have 6–10 members, additional teams from all areas of the organization may be formed to help the steering team plan and implement the changes.

In moving to a team-based organization, the steering team for change might naturally include the managers from each functional area as well as representatives from HR, quality, customer service, and the union leadership. This, of course, depends on the organization's current structure, purpose for moving to teams, focus for the teams, and expertise in moving to a team-based structure. Implementation teams may include groups focused on training and development, information management, financial management, rewards and recognition, and task-oriented pilot groups.

As a final note on creating the transition structure, we strongly recommend that the change steering team begin by developing their own high-performance teamwork skills. As with any major change initiative, a steering team will necessarily encounter many bumps along the road to success. Borrowing from the wisdom of noted change expert Rosabeth Moss Kanter, we agree that *every change initiative looks like and feels like a failure in the middle*. And so, when the going gets tough (and it always does), effective team management practices will help the steering group create their roadmap for change, adapt it as necessary, and keep people working collectively toward the change goals. Problem-solving skills will help the group think creatively to produce the required ingenuity, and conflict-handling protocols will help the group remain whole and focused on the task.

Transition Management: Identifying How Key Stakeholders and Power Groups Will Be Involved and Consulted

Change Energy: Who needs to be onside?

The job of the change leadership is to analyze the readiness to change of formal and informal power groups whose support and involvement are necessary to make the change goals happen.

We will now present a process for diagnosing the level of energy that key employees have for supporting the proposed change and for creating a plan to build their support and commitment.

Stakeholder Assessment

In moving to a team-based environment, there are many stakeholders whose support and commitment are essential to the process, including senior management, middle management, the union leadership, groups of employees, suppliers, and customers. If these groups are not involved and honored along the way, their resistance is almost inevitable. Here we look at two stakeholder groups whose needs are often overlooked or ignored when planning team-based structures in the organization. They are the union and middle management.

- ❖ **The Union.** If your organization is unionized and if an empowered workforce is part of your vision, it must be part of the union's vision as well. All too often, the change leadership makes the mistake of creating the vision first and including the union after. They then become angry and frustrated when the union does not buy into their vision. This approach does not work. For union support and commitment, the union must be an equal partner in understanding the reason for change, developing the vision, creating the action plans, and implementing the results.

- ❖ **Middle Managers.** Much has been written about the plight of the middle manager when it comes to implementing a team-based structure. For example, Bergmann and De Meuse (1996) and Hellinghausen and Myers (1998) point to the fact that middle managers and supervisors might present a barrier to implementing empowered teams. On the surface, it appears that the very concept of empowered teams poses a threat to their span of control and even their jobs.

We have observed that middle managers often find themselves between a rock and a hard place during the change to a team-based structure. On the one hand, they are the caretakers of the status quo, ensuring that operations run smoothly, quality and service are maintained, and promises are fulfilled. On the other hand, they are asked to allow valuable employees to attend information sessions, training programs, and team meetings, all which take away from their ability to keep the old system working. No wonder middle managers feel threatened, misunderstood, and undervalued during this transition process.

To build the support and commitment of these groups, the leadership needs to create two-way communications with them, treating their concerns and issues with respect. They may need additional resources, flexibility to increase overtime hours, or some latitude in scheduling to balance the needs of the two competing systems—the old and the new. Managers and supervisors also need to be fully informed as to why the change is necessary and to be involved in forming the vision, creating the transition process, identifying the priorities for action, and shaping their new roles.

With open communication, middle managers are equipped to play a pivotal role in leading and motivating their own employees to support the change. They need timely information from the change leadership so that they are fully informed of all new initiatives, understanding why the issue is important, what the solution is, and how they can help. As suggested by Larkin and Larkin (1996), employees prefer to hear about change from the person they are closest to, their direct supervisor.

A Team Tool for Assessing Support and Commitment

A helpful tool for assessing the support and commitment of each stakeholder group is one we adapted from Beckhard and Harris (1987). The tool helps change leaders identify the stakeholders impacted by the change, assess the level of support required of each stakeholder group, and then assess their actual commitment. The change team can then create a strategy to reduce the gap between the desired and actual commitment required for each group.

ASSESSING COMMITMENT

To bring about change, who (what stakeholders) need to be involved?

What role does each stakeholder group need to play to bring about the change?

❖ Let the change happen by not blocking the process?

❖ Help the change process by supporting and providing resources?

❖ Champion the change by actively leading and role modeling?

What role is each stakeholder group likely playing at the present time?

❖ Resistor: Opposing the change, either covertly or overtly?

❖ Bystander: Undecided about whether to support or oppose the change?

❖ Helper: Helping the process by supporting and providing resources?

❖ Champion: Actively leading the change and being a role model for others?

BUILDING SUPPORT

What is our plan for creating the necessary commitment and involvement?

❖ If they are resistors, do they need information or experience to create dissatisfaction with the status quo and a sense of urgency? What additional information or perspectives do they need to convince them of the wisdom of the change plan? How will you give it to them?

❖ If they are bystanders, are you providing the leadership and structure that they require? Is there a vision? Has the group been involved in creating it? Have they had an opportunity to discuss the vision with you? Have you created priorities for action? Have you set goals and initiated teams to work on those goals? Does the stakeholder group know how they can contribute to the vision, priorities, and goals? Have they received the necessary training and development to accomplish those goals?

❖ If they are helpers and champions, are you supporting their change initiatives and removing obstacles to their success? Do you have clear and open channels of communication?

Stakeholder Analysis

Stakeholders	Managers	Supervisors	Human Resources	Union Leadership	Employees
Champions	O	O			
Helpers	X	X	O	X O	
Bystanders			X		O
Resistors					X

X = present state with respect to the change

O = where this person or group needs to be

STEP #3: CREATE A COMMON
UNDERSTANDING OF WHY CHANGE IS NECESSARY

Creating a sense of urgency for change among a broad base of employees requires careful planning and perseverance. In many organizations experiencing turbulence, however, only the most senior managers understand that things are amiss. So although top management understands that major change is required, other groups in the organization may remain ignorant or indifferent.

A frank discussion sharing potentially unpleasant facts such as financial losses, decreasing market share, new entrants to the market, lack of revenue, and threatening industry trends is essential to helping people make their own assessment of the need to change (Kotter, 1996; Spector, 1989). All too often, leaders shelter employees from reality and sugarcoat their messages, fearing that the truth will paralyze the workforce or that competitive information will fall into the wrong hands. But a lack of pertinent information only serves to keep employees firmly rooted in the status quo. They do not have enough information to make educated assessments about why and how they must change. As Dannemiller and her colleagues (2000) reason, the purpose of sharing information with all of the stakeholders is to make them smart. A critical mass of smart, informed, and knowledgeable people make good decisions.

How Do You Create a Sense of Urgency?

To create a sense of urgency, identify what information key groups of employees need to understand and explore, as well as the credible sources for delivering the information. In moving to a team-based structure, the following examples may be relevant:

❖   **The CEO** sharing the organization's challenges, opportunities, strengths, and weaknesses. How has the current functional structure limited the organization's flexibility to act? How will teams improve innovation, speed to market, and communications?

❖   **An expert** on teams describing the potential benefits and pitfalls of moving to a team-based structure.

❖   **A valued customer** describing the customer's challenges and opportunities and how your organization must respond to help them achieve these new strategies. How has a team from your organization exceeded their expectations in the past? How has your organization failed to meet customer expectations? Did bureaucracy and politics get in the way of customer service? How does your organization need to consistently respond to retain existing business and gain new business?

❖ **A CFO** sharing financial metrics such as flat revenues, loss of market share, the opportunity cost of delays due to a lack of teamwork, and other costs associated with layers of bureaucracy.

While employees may not like the messages that they hear, they will appreciate the opportunity to learn about the state of their organization from reliable sources. In fact, we have found that when employees learn that things are amiss, they are eager to implement changes and question why management has been dragging its feet. When you begin to hear and feel this kind of momentum for change from a critical mass of employees, it is a sure sign that you have created a sense of urgency and that people are becoming energized to act.

STEP #4: CREATE AND COMMUNICATE A SHARED VISION FOR SUCCESS

Employees need to understand not only why there is a need for change but also what the organization wishes to become. The "what" is the vision, or a picture of the ideal future state. Developed by the steering team, often with the help of other important stakeholders, the vision determines and clarifies the direction in which the organization needs to move. It is in effect a clear and compelling statement of the change leadership's commitment to the future (Beckhard & Harris, 1987). The clearer the vision, the clearer the path to change.

There are several key activities that can help the steering team create an effective change vision. These are described in the following paragraphs.

Developing the Vision

The vision may be developed by the steering team only, or with the assistance of important stakeholder groups whose support is needed to implement the vision. Just as with Lewin's Iowa housewives, we've learned that the more people who have an opportunity to participate in shaping the vision, the greater the understanding and commitment to the vision. So even if the vision is drafted by a small group, the steering team should ensure that the broader organizational membership has an opportunity to "touch" the vision by giving their input and discussing how they may modify it to apply to their particular teams.

For processes on creating the vision, refer to Chapter 2, Planner Element #2, page 24.

Communicating the Vision
Clearly to Other Groups in the Organization

Perhaps the most important job of the steering team—once the vision has been created—is to communicate it clearly and often to other groups. We've learned that simply holding a meeting or sending out a memo describing the vision does little to create the understanding and support people need to actually implement the vision. People need an opportunity to hear about the vision firsthand from their change leaders and to discuss it. What excites them? What concerns them? How might they adapt to the vision? Real involvement, whereby people's hopes and fears are expressed and dealt with in a meaningful and honest way, helps create understanding, acceptance, and support.

Conveying the Correct Messages

Just as important as the process for communicating the vision is what is actually said. Often, the leader's message focuses solely on why the status quo is bad and why the change is good. What leaders do not address is which aspects of the status quo are effective and worth preserving and which aspects of the change may be negative or unknown. Employees fearing that effective processes and ideas will be discarded for no good reason are likely to become defensive and angry. Employees seeing major losses due to the change do not want to hear their leaders extolling the virtues of the vision.

When any change effort is announced, employees immediately make their own assessment of the benefits and drawbacks of the change, identifying what they will lose and what they will gain. If the leadership's messages do not also offer this same analysis, employees will assume that the change plan is superficial or that the leadership has something to hide.

Communicating the vision is not a one-time event; the initial communication is only the first step. Once the vision has been shared with other groups, their expectations will rise and they will be on the lookout for behaviors and actions that support the vision. Are leaders setting goals in alignment with the vision? Are projects being disbanded that are no longer relevant? Are employees being rewarded for teamwork? Are managers managing and leading in a way that is consistent with the new team-based structure?

When it comes to implementing teams, leadership actions speak louder than any vision statement posted on a wall. In one organization we worked with, the steering team painstakingly spent months communicating their vision of team empowerment to the masses, only to have the corporate leadership introduce a new absenteeism program. With the announcement of a control-oriented absenteeism program, time and energy were diverted from realizing the vision. Because the new program was incongruent with the vision, much of the work spent communicating it was for naught. We learned firsthand the importance of supporting verbal messages with action. Any diversions or incongruent actions serve only to cloud the message, and people simply don't know what to focus on.

STEP #5: DEVELOP AN INTEGRATED CHANGE PLAN WITH STRATEGIES, TACTICS, AND GOALS

Some people respond well to visioning. They "get it" right away and have an intuitive sense of what they need to do to make the change a reality. Others need more detail before they make the arduous journey from the present state to the future vision. Think of it metaphorically as taking a trip. Upon knowing the destination, some people prefer to just get into their cars and head out; they will adapt, ask directions, and have adventures along the way. Others won't leave home without detailed maps, hotel bookings, tourist information, emergency kits, and so on. Some of your employees are like that. They need to know the timelines, goals, milestones, measuring sticks, changes in reporting relationships, job descriptions, and so on, for the change to a team-based structure. Of course, it's almost impossible to work all this out at the beginning, but the more the change leadership can plan and create a detailed roadmap for change, the faster people are likely to move.

Creating Strategies, Tactics, and Goals

It is the job of the change leadership to formalize an integrated change plan, complete with goals, timelines, roles and responsibilities, and other structural and logistical details in consultation with stakeholders. Specific goals can then be set and activities assigned to teams and individuals for action.

In moving to a team-based organization, the change leadership's integration strategy may include answers to the following questions:

❖ What will the new team structure look like? How many teams will there be? What individuals or groups will the teams report to? What will the physical layout look like? Will everyone belong to a team or not?

❖ How will the teams be managed? Will there be leaders? Who will they be? How will they be selected? Will they be permanent or temporary?

❖ How will team goals be set?

❖ How will team results be monitored?

❖ How will the work of the various teams be aligned? How will the work between teams flow? How will teams receive and share important information? How will issues between teams be surfaced and resolved?

❖ How will teams be rewarded?

❖ How will team members be compensated?

❖ When will this change take place? How will the new systems and processes be phased in? Will there be pilot teams to act as trials?

Eliminating the Inevitable Barriers to Action

All too often, implementation teams operating outside of the formal hierarchy run into obstacles. Kotter (1996) likens these obstacles to an "elephant blocking the path." In many ways, transition teams are operating in no-man's land: The old systems and processes no longer apply, and the new have yet to be developed.

When moving to a team-based organization, the obstacles in the path are many; there may be rules or policies that no longer apply, narrowly defined job categories, or managers who refuse to support the change. An essential role for the change leadership is to remove those obstacles as they appear, firmly and forcefully. If the obstacles are not removed, the implicit message to employees is that *management is not committed to this change.* Sensing this message, employees do the smart thing—namely, nothing—believing that "this change too shall pass."

STEP #6: ALIGN STRUCTURES, PROCESSES, AND BEHAVIORS TO SUPPORT THE CHANGE

With experimentation, trial, and learning, implementation teams and pilot groups discover what works. Then, and only then, the change leadership can begin aligning systems and policies to support the new culture. Our research and practice indicate that when the following building blocks are put into place, teams receive the support and direction they need to operate in their new work environment.

Building Block #1: A Clear Purpose and Goals

A driving force behind any team is its goals. Teams need challenging goals, with a clear understanding of how accomplishing these goals will help the organization succeed and enhance competitiveness. Clear and motivating goals give the team a sense of urgency to achieve. They help answer the following questions: Why are we here? What is our purpose? Why is it necessary for us to succeed?

The essential role of the change leadership is to set a clear purpose and performance expectations for each team and then to hold them accountable for the results. To ensure that each team's purpose is clear, with goals and tasks focused on fostering organizational success, the following points should be clarified:

❖ Why was the team formed? What is the team's purpose?

❖ Why is it necessary for the team to succeed?

❖ What specific objectives are to be achieved? Identify the specific deliverables expected and dates for completion.

❖ Who are the team's stakeholders?

❖ What relationships must the team develop with other teams to be successful?

❖ What is the team's scope? What part of the workflow are they responsible for? How do their activities aid the whole?

Building Block #2: Protocols for Creating Alignment With Other Teams and Individuals

Perhaps the greatest challenge in moving to a team-based organization is coordinating the work of all the teams. If this alignment does not happen, the organization is in danger of creating a new form of "silo" mentality. Each team must understand how its goals and contributions combine with others to achieve organizational objectives. Recently we worked with an organization that did not spend the time and energy defining how the various teams should work together. Alas, when the organization introduced a new service delivery system, it became painfully apparent that each team was working with a different vision of who its customer was, how it should service the customer, who had authority for decision making, who was responsible for project planning, and who was responsible for implementation.

While each team had defined its own role and responsibilities in isolation, all of the teams had not developed joint goals and strategies, nor had they defined how they would work together. As a result, the research and development group created a state-of-the-art system that the service delivery teams were not ready to deliver. The teams' failure to communicate, even when major problems arose, caused much frustration and anger. With the anger came blaming and finger-pointing, which in turn stifled meaningful communication. The result was missed deadlines and unhappy customers. Only when the team leaders regrouped and formed a cross-functional project-planning group to coordinate the efforts of all the teams did the project get back on track.

To avoid this kind of fiasco, we highly recommend that the roles, responsibilities, and working relationships between teams be defined early and often, as conditions vary. In the design phase, the change leadership should create a structural mechanism to coordinate the efforts of all teams. So, for example, all team leaders may be asked to form a committee to ensure coordination and alignment between teams. Alternatively, each team may be asked to appoint a partnering champion whose role is to liaise and coordinate with the other teams. The roles, responsibilities, and authority of those responsible for alignment must be clearly defined. They need to understand their authority to make decisions and change policy, their role in problem solving, and their responsibility to remove barriers.

The change leadership should also ask each team to create a partnering protocol to foster efficient and effective communication among teams. The partnering protocol works best when it is renewed for each new initiative where two or more teams share joint objectives. With enhanced communication and working relationships between the key players of a joint project, goals are more likely to be achieved efficiently and on time. In the following section, we offer a sample process for creating a partnering protocol.

THE PARTNERING PROTOCOL

1. Ask each team to identify the goals it has in common with other teams.

2. For each of the major goals, ask the key players involved from each team to meet to discuss the following:

   ❖ What are the goals that we have in common?

   ❖ For each shared goal, what are the activities that need to be undertaken to achieve it?

   ❖ Who is involved in carrying out the activities to achieve the goal and what are their roles?

3. When issues arise and disagreements occur, how will we surface and resolve them?

4. What will our norms and working protocols be? For example,

   ❖ How often will we meet to discuss issues and progress?

   ❖ Who will be responsible for organizing these meetings?

   ❖ How will we make decisions?

   ❖ How will we ensure that all views are heard and respected?

5. How will cost or resource savings, if any, be distributed?

6. How will rewards for goal completion be distributed?

7. Who will be responsible for communicating our issues and progress to other key stakeholders? What will our communication processes be?

8. What parts of our products and services need to conform to overall organizational standards, and what can be different?

9. How can we achieve synergies among teams? For example, what technologies or innovations should we share or incorporate into all team products and services?

The answers to these important questions form your partnering protocol. Partnering works because it promotes communication, joint goal setting, joint planning, and creative problem solving between teams. With better communication, issues are surfaced and raised before they become major problems or turn into personal conflicts.

Building Block #3: Clearly Defining Authority

A critical early step in the formation of a new team is the setting of team boundaries for responsibility, authority, and reporting requirements. Teams that do not have clear boundaries may experience great confusion, frustration, and disappointment as they learn the hard way that they have overstepped their limits. It's best to set and negotiate clear boundaries right at the start. These boundaries should not be static. As teams gain experience and expertise, they will become ready for more authority and responsibility. To define the team's authority, ask the following questions:

❖ What is the team's level of decision-making authority? In what areas do they have full authority to make autonomous decisions? In what areas must they consult with others? In what areas must they defer to others?

❖ Is the team to make a decision or a recommendation, provide information, or comply with management decisions?

❖ Specifically, whom does the team report to? At what milestones should the team report results and how should the results be reported?

❖ What are the nonnegotiable requirements or rules the team is expected to adhere to (e.g., spending limitations, legislative framework, process limitations, policies)?

❖ What is the empowerment schedule? How will more authority gradually be transferred to the team?

Building Block #4: Rewards Consistent With Team Objectives

Rewards communicate what behaviors the organization desires. To create support for teamwork, the change leadership must identify and reward behaviors and results that are consistent with team success.

Each stakeholder group, including managers, supervisors, the union, groups of employees, and the teams themselves, should be recognized and rewarded for the important role that they play. So if managers are coaching teams and removing barriers to their success, these behaviors should be recognized. If supervisors have rearranged the workflow so that key employees are free to participate in team meetings, they should also be recognized. If individuals volunteer to facilitate or train teams, they too should be rewarded. And of course, each team should be recognized for the important contribution that it makes.

Rewards and recognition can take many forms, and our belief is that a representative group of all stakeholders should be created to design a meaningful reward and recognition system. While some theorists believe that "empowered employees must be compensated for their increased responsibility and accountability," other research suggests that financial rewards are often not necessary or expected (for example, Hellinghausen & Myers, 1998). These authors suggest that recognition and appreciation, such as a dinner out with the CEO, a personal congratulations from a senior manager, or an article in the company newsletter, can serve to provide the necessary recognition.

Building Block #5: Access to Information

Teams need access to relevant information. For employees to be more involved in the functioning of the organization, they must have access to the same critical information the leadership has to problem-solve and plan.

To provide effective information, ask the following questions:

❖ Does the team have ready access to the information and knowledge that members need to select the appropriate strategy or approach for tackling the task?

❖ Does the team have access to all the information, expertise, and data they need to make good decisions?

❖ Does the team have free and frequent access to the senior team to check data, share insights, and check assumptions so that they are working with the best available data?

❖ Is the team in constant contact with their customers and stakeholders to ensure they have the most up-to-date information and perspectives?

❖ Does the team have access to knowledge from other teams?

Perhaps no other management act has the leverage that opening up the channels of communication can provide. Sharing critical information about the organization's goals, progress, and challenges gives employees the knowledge and perspectives they need to truly add value. It not only helps the change leaders maintain a sense of urgency but also helps employees see the results of their hard work paying off. Employees who have full access to company information feel trusted, valued, and responsible for acting on the information to make good decisions.

Building Block #6: Training

Working in a team-based organization requires different skills, abilities, and attitudes than working within a functional hierarchy. Skills such as problem solving, conflict handling, facilitating meetings, communicating nondefensively, listening, performing statistical analysis, and solving quality problems are required competencies. Providing employees with the proper training to excel in their new roles will enhance their competence and confidence to succeed.

Building Block #7: Technological, Material, and People Resources

Teams need myriad resources to accomplish their goals, including tools, supplies, raw materials, appropriate membership, appropriate technology, access to data and information, access to expert opinion and knowledge, and the time to complete their assignments.

Higher management is responsible for ensuring that the team has the resources and people power it needs to succeed. A realistic appraisal of the resources required will go a long way toward helping the team understand that the organization is committed to its success. To ensure adequate resources, ask the following questions:

❖ What material resources does the team need to accomplish its purpose and goals? How will we make these resources available?

❖ Do members have the requisite skill, ability, and experience to deliver on the performance expectations? What additional expertise does the team need to be successful? How can we provide training and learning experiences to develop the requisite skills and ability?

❖ What subject matter experts can we make available to share their knowledge and expertise?

❖ Realistically, when does the team need to have its tasks completed? How can we staff the team so it can meet its deadlines?

❖ What technology does the team need access to? How can we provide access?

STEP #7: CONSOLIDATE IMPROVEMENTS AND PRODUCE MORE CHANGE

In the mid-1500s, after 14 years of Elizabethan rule, the dukes of northern England joined forces in an attempt to overthrow Queen Elizabeth and replace her with a new queen, Mary, Queen of Scots. The northern dukes who were deeply committed to Catholicism resented Queen Elizabeth's Protestant rule and wished to return England to Catholicism. Queen Elizabeth, taking decisive action, was able to stop the revolt and capture her enemies, ordering them all to death by hanging.

Queen Elizabeth's predicament teaches change leaders a powerful lesson. Never assume that the momentum for change will keep growing without constant leadership attention and focus. Even though the change implementation may be well under way—as Elizabeth's reign of 14 years was—old patterns of behavior may quickly reemerge if the leadership does not stay focused and attentive. Throughout the change, employees will be watching for signs that leadership support and commitment are waning. If they suspect leadership support is lacking, all progress may halt or even regress.

In one organization that we worked with, despite a full year of fruitful progress, the change goals were thwarted when the change champion was promoted to another position. To make matters worse, the corporate leadership implemented a new initiative that served to divert management's energy and focus from driving the change. These unfortunate occurrences served to delay the change, and at the time of writing we are waiting to see if the steering team can regain their momentum.

This momentum is difficult to sustain. Change agents often lose interest in a project once it is planned and appears to be running smoothly. But like Queen Elizabeth's reign, our change projects are in danger of coming to a premature end if we forget to keep monitoring, evaluating, and fine-tuning them.

STEP #8: INTEGRATE THE CHANGE INTO THE CULTURE AND INSTITUTIONALIZE NEW APPROACHES

Culture defines "how we do things around here." Culture is like the air that we breathe; it is all around us, defining our habitual, taken-for-granted beliefs and behaviors. When these practices are challenged we know right away because we feel awkward, unsettled, or even angry.

While the formal change to a team-based structure may take place over a defined period of time, it takes much more time before people adapt to the new culture. A friend of ours tells the story about his family's recent move to highlight the difference between structural change and the successful adoption of a new culture. The physical move from his family home to another house a few blocks away took one weekend. On Friday morning they began the move, and by Sunday evening they were relocated in their new house with most boxes unpacked. Even though the physical move had taken place, each member of the family was still experiencing the transition; they still missed their old house, and it took his wife well over 6 months to actually call the new house a home and to become settled into the new neighborhood.

And so it goes with any change. While employees may be physically assigned to a new team with a new leader and new roles and responsibilities, it often takes more time before employees truly adjust to their new work culture. It takes time for old habits and working styles to die and new ones to become the norm.

Management's greatest challenge at this stage of the process is to patiently and persistently reinforce the expectations of the new culture. So, for example, some employees may be reluctant at first to accept authority or take on responsibility, despite their new job description. Others will defer to their former leaders until they become comfortable with the new regime. Still others will find it difficult to share information that traditionally was not shared. Members of one team we worked with were loath to receive financial statements, claiming that only the leadership should have such information. These members were simply not accustomed to receiving data about their organization's financial status and reported that they did not want the responsibility associated with knowing the reality of their competitive business environment.

By consistently role modeling and reinforcing new norms and behaviors, leaders help employees complete their transition to their new work environment. Over time, employees settle in and become accustomed to *the new ways that we do things around here*; they adapt to their new culture.

Exercises: Contents

CHAPTER 1

EXERCISE 1.1: TEAM EFFECTIVENESS GAP ANALYZER

Teams can do an overall diagnostic using our Team Effectiveness Model Gap Analyzer to obtain an overview of areas of most and least effectiveness.

Team Effectiveness Model Gap Analyzer

Level	Team Management Practices	Problem Solving	Conflict Handling
4 Ready ("Watch our dust!")	Team purpose and goals are clearly defined and compelling and our whole team is focused on achieving them. Members are working collectively, tapping the full potential of all and creating superior results. We have a well-defined approach for tackling our challenges and it is working for us. Relationships with key stakeholders are well defined, productive, and focused on the overall goals. Our team norms are well established and everybody abides by them. All individuals are included and respected as full, contributing members. All members are fully committed to the team and its purpose.	Our team creates ingenious "1 + 1 > 2" solutions. We use communication patience skills to foster dialogue, share important knowledge, and explore assumptions. We use synergy tools to help members expand their thinking, generate and build on ideas, and evaluate those ideas to arrive at superior solutions. We use the right process tools to guide our work. We discuss and agree upon sound approaches to problem solving, and we collect the relevant information before jumping into discussions about solutions.	We have established a team climate that welcomes and accepts diverse points of view, and our members feel safe to express themselves fully. We understand that conflict is a normal and natural part of team life. When conflicts do occur, we pause and discuss how we can move forward. We then develop a protocol to help us prevent similar conflicts in the future. We do not allow conflict to become personalized.
3 Getting Ready ("We're on the right track")	Team purpose and goals are becoming clear. The team is on the right track for completing our purpose, vision, priorities, and goals. Members are committed to working collectively, and we are learning how to tap into the full potential of all. We are defining/tweaking our approach for tackling our challenges, and more often than not, the approach is working for us. Results are coming nicely. Relationships with key stakeholders are well defined and for the most part are working. We are establishing team norms. Most of the time we are unafraid to confront difficulties and to discuss ways of working together more productively. Commitment to the team is fairly high.	Our team is learning how to create breakthrough "1 + 1 > 2" solutions. When we use communication patience and synergy tools, we arrive at superior solutions. Our process tools are helping guide our work and expand our creative thinking. We are beginning to be disciplined about how we approach problem solving and have put more structure around our discussions.	We're working hard to promote a team climate that welcomes diverse views so that members feel safe to express themselves. When conflicts do occur, we pause and discuss how we can move forward.

(Continued)

(Continued)

Level	Team Management Practices	Problem Solving	Conflict Handling
2 Moving Slowly ("We're not on track yet")	Loosely defined goals provide some focus and direction. We're beginning to recognize that a clear purpose and vision are important. We recognize that we are not tapping the full potential of all, and as a result, we're not producing the results expected of us. We do not have the right approach or strategy for tackling our challenges, and this is slowing us down. Experience has taught us that we need to foster relationships with key stakeholders. We're beginning to identify, clarify, and develop relationships with key groups. Team norms are loosely defined. Sometimes we do not live up to the great ideas that we had initially discussed for working together. Commitment of some members to the team is uneven.	Our team creates "1 + 1 = 2" solutions. Our team meetings are focused on sharing information from each member's area of responsibility. We do not use processes and techniques to identify common challenges, share relevant information, build on each other's ideas, or generate solutions that benefit all members and stakeholders. At best, we operate as a group instead of a real team. We are not disciplined in our problem-solving approach, and our discussions seem at times to be going in circles. We do not base our discussions nearly enough on sound information, but rather on members' opinions and intuitions.	Our team climate does not always welcome diverse views, and members are often uncomfortable with expressing their thoughts and feelings. We have no protocols in place to help us manage conflict effectively. As a result, conflicts often steer us off track and block us from moving forward.
1 Stalled ("We are spinning our wheels")	We have no concept of our purpose or vision. We do not have a useful approach or strategy for tackling our challenges, and this is slowing us down. Roles and responsibilities are unclear, resulting in confusion and frustration. Relationships with key stakeholder groups are unclear or not viewed as important. Team norms do not exist. People disagree over how we should be working together, and conflict is glossed over or ignored. Some members are not committed to the team at all.	Our team creates "1 + 1 < 2" solutions. Our team meetings are chaotic, with members interrupting, grandstanding, withholding information, and so on. Our inability to generate workable solutions stops progressive action and blocks people from moving forward on important issues.	Our team climate does not welcome diverse views and members do not feel safe to express themselves. We have no protocols in place to help us manage conflict effectively. As a result, conflicts often steer us off track and block us from moving forward. Members have personalized the conflicts, and cliques have formed to create "we–they" separations.

Other exercises referenced in Chapter 1: For diagnostics that focus on each of the three key vital signs of team effectiveness, see the Team Management Practices Assessment, page 117, and the Team Problem-Solving Assessment, page 145.

CHAPTER 2
EXERCISE 2.1: TEAM MANAGEMENT PRACTICES ASSESSMENT

OBJECTIVES

To assess the strength of your team's team management practices.

To determine helpful processes your team needs to put in place to enhance the way you work together.

TIME REQUIRED

1 hour to complete assessment and discuss

BACKGROUND

See Chapter 2, "Creating Smart Team Management Practices."
This assessment can be used periodically with your team to assess your development and use of effective team management practices.

MATERIALS REQUIRED

Copies of the Team Management Practices Assessment

STEPS

1. Distribute copies of the Team Management Practices Assessment.

2. Ask each member to contribute individually. Explain that the assessments will be reviewed collectively to show the team's combined perspective.

3. Share the range of responses for each question. Ask participants to discuss why they answered the way they did, particularly where most members responded with "No."

4. Identify the team management practices that need improvement. Discuss ways to improve each area requiring work.

5. **Discussion Question:** What processes can we put in place to enhance each area that was identified as needing improvement?

Team Management Practices Assessment

Team Task Processes	Yes	No
1. Do our team members have a deep understanding of the forces compelling the need for change or continuous improvement?	☐	☐
2. Does our team have a clearly defined purpose statement, which we often refer to for guidance?	☐	☐
3. Does our team have a well-defined description of its end state—a description of what will be different once the team has fulfilled its purpose?	☐	☐
4. Has our team developed clear goals with specific deliverables and dates for completion?	☐	☐
5. Does our team discuss and agree on the strategies for acquiring knowledge and accomplishing tasks before beginning the work?	☐	☐
6. Does our team understand its boundaries (the givens it must adhere to) and its scope?	☐	☐

Team Social Processes

	Yes	No
7. Does our group actively include all members as part of the team?	☐	☐
8. Do our members abide by respectful team norms?	☐	☐
9. Do members feel safe to be themselves and to share their honest opinions?	☐	☐
10. Do members take the initiative to offer their ideas, reservations, and feelings?	☐	☐
11. Do all members share leadership roles as required?	☐	☐
12. Are members' talents and expertise fully recognized and used?	☐	☐
13. Is our group creative in its approach to problem solving? Are we open to new ideas and do we constantly experiment with new ways of doing things?	☐	☐
14. Do members challenge and evaluate all proposals and solutions? Does the team encourage all members to offer their ideas?	☐	☐
15. Does our team have the right composition of membership skills and experience?	☐	☐
16. Are our meetings efficient and effective? Do we make sure our time is not wasted?	☐	☐
17. Does each member have an equal voice?	☐	☐

Commitment to the Team

	Yes	No
18. Does our team demand that everyone contribute fully, especially over the long term?	☐	☐
19. Does each member assume personal responsibility for getting our work done?	☐	☐
20. Are team norms for confidentiality negotiated and adhered to?	☐	☐
21. Do members complete team work assignments?	☐	☐
22. Do members take on extra work when necessary to ensure that goals are met?	☐	☐
23. Are all members committed to this group and its purpose?	☐	☐

Exercise 2.2: Marvin's Trends Mind Map

OBJECTIVES

To create a shared understanding of the myriad trends impacting the team's reason for being.

TIME REQUIRED

2 hours +

BACKGROUND

See Chapter 2, "Creating Smart Team Management Practices."

Once team members map the many and varied trends impacting their team's purpose, they can identify which trends and challenges they want to tackle with their team. The mind map helps ground the group in the real challenges that they face as a team and an organization.

MATERIALS REQUIRED

Blank poster paper taped on a large flat wall. Ideally, the writing surface should be at least 5 feet wide and 4 feet high.

Many different colors of markers so that ideally you have one color for each trend identified.

At least two people to facilitate the exercise: one recorder of the trends on the mind map and one facilitator to encourage responses.

STEPS

1. Create the mind map by writing the team's purpose in the center of the map and placing a circle around it. For example, the team's purpose may be "to improve the quality of our products and services" or "to enhance work and family balance at our facility."

2. Ask all members to step over to the mind map. To encourage involvement, ask all members to remain standing and to gather around so that they are close to the map and to each other.

3. Explain that you will be creating a map of all the trends in your organization, both internal and external, that are impacting your challenge or purpose statement.

4. Explain the following rules:
   - ❖ Call out your trends, indicating where they should go on the map by stating that they are either new trends or subtrends of trends that have already been mapped. As the trends are called out, the facilitator will ask the member if the trend is a new trend or a subtrend. The participant will answer, and the trend will be drawn on the map accordingly. Ideally, each new trend will be in a separate color to differentiate the trends. A title or brief identifier of the trend is written along the trend line as well.
   - ❖ To encourage ownership and participation, it is very important to enforce the following ground rule: The person who volunteered the trend is the person who identifies where it should go on the map (either a new trend or a subtrend). Other members should not take responsibility for trends that they did not identify.
   - ❖ No evaluation. If a member identifies a trend, it is a trend and it is recorded on the map. Do not allow other members to censor each other's ideas. In most instances, there will be conflicting trends identified, such as "need for improved quality control" and "need for greater flexibility in our processes." These dilemmas are real and should be recorded for the team to wrestle with at a later stage.

5. Encourage members to offer all possible trends, identifying trends that are both external and internal to the organization.

6. Once all of the trends have been identified, circle each trend (main trend and subtrends) and discuss. Encourage members to explain what they meant and to share their diverse perspectives.

7. Following the discussion, ask each member to priority vote on trends that they believe are the most important for their team to tackle. Give each member five votes. Tally the votes to determine which trends the team believes are the most important to tackle first.

AN ADDITIONAL STEP

Ask the team to assess the relative importance of each trend by placing each trend in the following matrix:

- ❖ Effort required (easy vs. hard)
- ❖ Payoff (high vs. low)

According to the payoff matrix, the team will focus on the trends and challenges that will give them the highest return for the smallest effort required.

8. Review the list and discuss whether it makes sense. Are there other trends that should be addressed first?

9. The team has now identified the most important and relevant trends and challenges they must address to be successful.

EXERCISE 2.3: DEFINING OUR TEAM PURPOSE

OBJECTIVES

To create a meaningful and relevant team purpose.

TIME REQUIRED

2 hours +

BACKGROUND

See Chapter 2, "Creating Smart Team Management Practices."

This exercise is designed to tap why the team is important to each team member, from a business and personal point of view, and to create a common purpose that all members can commit to. Ideally this exercise is preceded by the Mind Map.

MATERIALS REQUIRED

Copies of the Our Team Purpose questions for each participant

STEPS

1. Distribute copies of the exercise, Our Team Purpose.

2. Ask each member to silently reflect on the questions and to record their answers in the space provided. Allow 15 minutes for personal reflection.

3. Give each member 5 minutes of uninterrupted time to share his or her answers. Be sure to ask all members to listen fully to the person speaking. It is very important that each member has time to share his or her personal responses without interruption or evaluation.

4. Ask members to reflect on what was similar in the reflections that they heard. Record these similarities and discuss. Ask members to reflect on what was different in the reflections that they heard. Record these differences and discuss.

5. From these similarities and differences, create a shared team purpose that all members can commit to:

   So, given all that, the overall purpose of our team is . . .

   Collect ideas on a flipchart, asking members to give a full explanation. Group common statements and discuss fully until the group arrives at a common purpose statement.

   Ideally, the mission statement is a short, concise statement that speaks volumes.

6. Review the mission statement with the team sponsor and key stakeholders for their input. Adapt as necessary.

Our Team Purpose

Silently reflect on the following questions, and record your responses in the space provided.

1. What are the key challenges that we face with respect to this initiative? Data from the Trends Mind Map are relevant here.

2. Given our Mind Map or other discussions, what challenges do you want to tackle with this team?

3. Why does this team need to succeed?

4. When we succeed, what unique contributions will we make?

5. Who are our key stakeholders? What purpose will we serve for them?

6. Why is this team's success important to you?

7. Given all that, what is our purpose for being?

Exercise 2.4: Developing Team Vision and Strategy

OBJECTIVES

To create a shared understanding of the team's ideal solution, from which you will develop reality-based priorities.

TIME REQUIRED

This exercise is best conducted in two sessions to allow some processing time between the process of creating the ideal scenario and refining priorities.

Session one—3 hours +

Session two—2 hours +

BACKGROUND

See Chapter 2, Planner Element #2: Creating Your Team's Vision & Strategy—The Ideal "What"

Teams need to free themselves from the constraints of the present reality to create winning possibilities for their future. Once team members create their ideal scenario, they need to assess the elements of their vision for reality and develop a series of priorities that will move them forward.

Consider involving your team's sponsor, customers, and other stakeholders in this exercise. Their insights and perspectives will be invaluable.

MATERIALS REQUIRED

Dependent upon your process. Many groups choose from flipcharts, markers, musical instruments, paint, Lego and other building toys, acting props, and so on.

STEPS

Session One

1. Ask your team to silently imagine their ideal scenario, one in which they have achieved their mission.

To foster their thinking, ask the following questions:

- ❖ What goals will we have accomplished?
- ❖ What impact will we have made on our organization?
- ❖ In what ways have we satisfied the needs of our stakeholders?
- ❖ What processes, procedures, and systems are now in place?
- ❖ How have we added value?
- ❖ What new skills and expertise have we acquired? How?
- ❖ What does it feel like to be part of the team?
- ❖ How have our roles changed?

To tap their creative spirit, we often offer one of the following scenarios for the team to adopt, as they reflect on the above questions:

- ❖ Imagine your team is on the cover of *Fortune* as a model success story. What does the article say about your great success?
- ❖ Write a letter to your organization's founder about your team's success. What accomplishments will you tell him or her about?
- ❖ Imagine that you have been away from your team on a special assignment for 3–5 years. As you rejoin the team on a catch-up meeting, what accomplishments will they tell you about?
- ❖ Imagine you are flying in a helicopter over your organization's building(s) and that you can see through the roofs into the many offices, hallways, and rooms (you have special goggles on). What do you see?

2. Collect member ideas and record on a flipchart. Depending on the scenario you adopt, give team members time to create their letter, magazine article, or helicopter ride. Many teams like to act out, draw, or perform their visions. Typically, as teams let go of their inhibitions, they tap into a source of creative energy and have a lot of fun.

3. Ask members to present their vision. Following the presentation, allow and encourage questions of understanding, but do not allow criticism or judgment.

4. Ask the team to identify key themes from the vision. Record on a flipchart.

5. Have a reality dialogue. Now is the time for the team to impose reality on the discussion. The team members and sponsors—ideally with the input of key stakeholders—must discuss what short-term and long-term priorities they are willing and able to commit to achieving.

6. Prioritize these items from high to low using appropriate criteria, such as importance, payoff, benefit, impact, cost, and time. Categorize the priorities into phase-one, phase-two, or phase-three priorities.

Session Two

1. Post the priorities from session one and review and discuss. Ask a series of questions to help the team test their thinking. Do these priorities make sense to you? Can we commit to achieving the phase-one priorities right away? If we put the phase-two and phase-three priorities on the back burner right now, will we suffer? Do these priorities make sense to our customers? How will achieving these priorities improve the health of our business? Modify the priorities as directed by the group.

2. Ask the group to identify the present thinking and behaviors that may block them from achieving their priorities. Record their ideas on a flipchart. Discuss each idea fully and ask for examples of how this thinking has limited the range of responses to team-related problems.

3. Now ask members to discuss what patterns of thinking and behavior they must create for their vision and priorities to become reality. To foster discussion, ask the following questions: What new habits do we need to create? What assumptions should we hold for customer service, quality, or innovation? How will we know whether we are on track? What behaviors do we need to reinforce, and what processes and systems will we put in place to reward them?

Your team now has well-defined priorities and has discussed the thinking and behaviors it must adopt to achieve meaningful change.

Many teams like to post or display their vision as a constant reminder of their ideal future. Visions can be displayed as posters, collages, songs, poems, and statues. The more creative, the better.

EXERCISE 2.5: DEVELOPING CLEAR, MOTIVATING GOALS AND ACCOUNTABILITIES

OBJECTIVES

To create goals and strategies for achieving your team's priorities.

To identify specific results by which the team will measure its success and for which it will hold itself accountable.

TIME REQUIRED

2 hours +

BACKGROUND

See Chapter 2, "Creating Smart Team Management Practices."

MATERIALS REQUIRED

It is useful to begin with the team's mission, vision, and priorities.

Copies of the Goal Statement Form for each team member

STEPS

1. Begin with the team priorities you developed when you created your mission and vision. By starting here, your team's goals will be aligned with your mission and vision and with the overall goals of your organization.

2. Select your first team priority and set goals to accomplish it by answering the following questions:
   ❖ What are the specific objectives to be achieved?
   ❖ What specific results or deliverables are expected of us? By whom?

3. Assess goals to make sure that they meet the following SMART criteria: Are they specific, meaningful, achievable, relevant, and trackable?

4. Make action plans. Ask members to specify how the goals will be achieved, who will be responsible for each activity, and the dates for completion by answering the following:
   ❖ What process or strategy will we use to achieve our goal?
   ❖ What key activities are required? By whom?
   ❖ What are the expected dates for completion of each activity?

5. Complete an action planning relevance test by asking team members to consider how each action will help them accomplish their goal. If it does not meet the test, revise it or abandon it if you can.

6. Take action.

7. Monitor progress and self-correct. Be sure to be open to the feedback of your sponsors, stakeholders, and customers. As their realities change, yours will too.

8. Assessing progress and monitoring feedback are critical activities. To ensure that you build them into your action planning, establish the following:

❖ Specific times at which your performance will be reviewed. Think about how you will measure success and who will be involved in the process.

❖ Milestones for reporting results. Who will you report your results to? What information and metrics will be helpful to them?

Goal Statement Form

Goal: Specify a clear goal or objective. What specific results do you want to achieve?

Make sure your goal can be characterized as follows:

Specific—Is it clear? Can your team members understand it?

Meaningful—Will you pursue this goal with enthusiasm and commitment?

Achievable—Do you have the resources you need? Is this the right time to be focusing on this goal?

Relevant—Will achieving this goal accomplish the intended business result?

Trackable—Is the result measurable in terms that all team members can track?

Our goal:

Relationship to our team's mission:

Activities	Responsibility	Timing	Measurement
How will you accomplish the goal? What specific activities will each member undertake?	Who will commit to achieving the activity and how? Refer to the following question about responsibility.	By what date will each member agree to have his or her activities completed?	How will you track the effectiveness of each activity and the results?

AUTHORITY

With respect to this goal:

A = Authority   Who has the authority to make decisions? The goal leader? The team? Others?

R = Responsibility   Who has responsibility for a particular action (but not necessarily authority)?

S = Support   Who will be involved in a support role? What will that involvement entail?

C = Consulted   Who should be consulted?

I = Informed   Who should be informed?

Boundaries   What processes, laws, rules, or legislation must the team abide by in accomplishing the goal?

EXERCISE 2.6: NEGOTIATING
AUTHORITY WITH YOUR TEAM SPONSOR

OBJECTIVES

Most teams develop their purpose, priorities, and goals in response to an opportunity designated by a team sponsor, usually higher management. Once teams have had an opportunity to research and explore their challenge, this exercise gives team members an opportunity to clarify their initiative's scope, boundaries, and the overall authority they have to make change.

TIME REQUIRED

1–2 hours +

MATERIALS REQUIRED

Conversation Starters: Negotiating Authority With Your Team Sponsor

STEPS

1. Invite your team sponsor to a meeting to explore purpose and performance expectations. Provide ample time for dialogue, as this is an important opportunity for members to ask questions and to develop a working understanding of their scope, boundaries, and decision-making latitude. Specifically, we recommend that the conversations address the following:
    *   The team's expected contribution to the organization's mission and strategy
    *   A clear purpose and performance expectations for the team
    *   An understanding of the team's authority
    *   A reward strategy
    *   Access to information
    *   Access to resources
    *   Access to training and consultation

2. Team members are also developing an important relationship with their sponsor and should discuss communication expectations (How often do we need to communicate? What vehicles will we use? Who is responsible?).

Conversation Starters: Negotiating Authority With Your Team Sponsor

Conversations	*Agreements*
Our overall challenge and how it relates to organizational success:	
Our priorities for action:	
The overall project scope:	
Boundaries and givens that we must adhere to (legislation, budget, resources, etc.):	
Decision-making latitude (refer to the Authority Ladder):	
Access to resources (human, technical, financial, and training):	
Expected deadline for completion:	
Deliverables expected:	
Reporting requirements (milestones, communications methods, and frequency):	
Expected rewards for project completion:	

Authority Ladder
_____

⬚ **Empowered**   The team has full authority to decide and is fully
accountable. Management is informed on a need-to-know basis.

⬚ **Decide Together**   Management and the team make these
decisions together.

⬚ **Generate Options**   Higher management has authority to decide
here; however, the team develops, assesses, and shares viable
options.

⬚ **Tell**   The team carries out higher management's solution. Higher
management has authority and is accountable.

EXERCISE 2.7: DEFINING TEAM MEMBERSHIP AND CONTRIBUTION

OBJECTIVES

To make sure you have the right mix of skills, experience, and leadership on the team to achieve your team purpose and goals.

TIME REQUIRED

1 hour +

BACKGROUND

See Chapter 2, Planner Element #5: Establishing Team Membership and Contribution.

MATERIALS REQUIRED

It is useful to begin with the team's mission, vision, and priorities.

Copies of the Team Member Selection Guide for each team member

It is helpful to create an overhead of the Team Member Selection Guide for the team to create together.

STEPS

1. Hand out copies of the Team Member Selection Guide, with the team mission or purpose and goals stated at the top of the page.

2. Brainstorm all the possible skills and expertise required for the team to achieve its mission and goals. Use multivoting or discussion to arrive at the 8–10 key skills that the team needs to be successful. List these skills in the space provided on the form. *Multivoting* is a quick and efficient tool for helping the team sort and prioritize ideas for consideration. After a list of ideas has been generated, usually via brainstorming, members vote with their feet, as they are each given five to seven dots or check marks to place beside the ideas they prefer. The ideas receiving the most votes are circled. The process is repeated until the group has identified a workable number of items. The great value of this tool is that it helps the group focus discussion on the ideas that are most important to the group.

3. List possible team member names on the appropriate space on the form.

4. Assess which skills each member brings to the team, and record.

5. If members lack skills and abilities, ask the following questions: What subject matter experts are available to the team to share their expertise? Who, with training and development, can build the requisite skills and ability?

6. Develop an action plan for securing the appropriate team membership and expertise.

ADAPTATION

Often teams are formed on the basis of an existing structure or unit. In this situation, this exercise can be very useful for identifying training and development plans for team members and/or to identify experts who can offer technical advice not available on the team.

Team Member Selection Guide

Team Purpose:

Team Goals:

Team Members [List names]	Skills and Expertise Required [Identify skills team needs]						

EXERCISE 2.8: RESOURCES
EACH MEMBER CONTRIBUTES TO THE TEAM

OBJECTIVES

To help members identify and share the skills, experiences, and attributes that they bring to the team.

TIME REQUIRED

1 hour +

BACKGROUND

See Chapter 2, Planner Element #5: Establishing Team Membership and Contribution.

MATERIALS REQUIRED

Copies of the Team Member Contribution Form for each member

STEPS

1. Explain that we all bring special resources to the team. Give some examples, such as education, skills, perspectives, and character qualities. Share that it is very important for team members to acknowledge the gifts that each person brings to the team so that we can all operate from a base of sufficiency—a belief that I'm okay and so are you.

2. Ask team members to silently reflect on the gifts and talents that they contribute to the team by completing the Team Member Contribution Form.

3. Instruct team members to sit facing each other in a circle; give each member 3–5 minutes of uninterrupted time to share their shield. Be sure to ask all members to listen fully to the person speaking. It is very important that each member has time to share his or her personal responses without interruption or evaluation.

VARIATIONS

❖ This exercise can be given as an individual exercise, whereby members do not share their reflections with the group.

❖ After completing steps 1 and 2, members can be paired and asked to share their answers with each other to receive positive confirmation and feedback from each other.

Team Member Contribution Form

Every member has gifts and talents they contribute to the team. Silently reflect on what you bring to the team and then create your personal shield below.

1. Skill(s) that I contribute to this team are . . .

2. Character qualities that I bring to this team are . . .

3. Experiences that I bring to this team include . . .

4. A unique perspective that I contribute to this team is . . .

5. Some contributions that I am making or have made include . . .

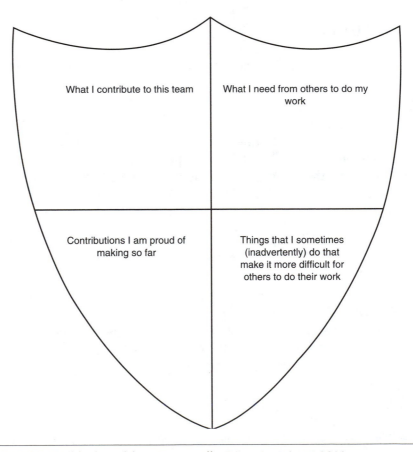

SOURCE: Shield adapted from Dannemiller Tyson Associates, 2000.

EXERCISE 2.9: TEAM CULTURE AUDIT

OBJECTIVES

To give team members the opportunity and permission to talk about how they think good team members should behave. Members make their implicit assumptions about effective member behavior explicit so that they can arrive at a shared understanding of effective team norms and protocols.

TIME REQUIRED

1 hour +

BACKGROUND

See Chapter 2, Planner Element #6: Norms and Protocols for Working Collectively.

MATERIALS REQUIRED

Copies of the Team Culture Audit for each member

Flipchart papers posted on the wall, each paper with one statement from the Team Culture Audit, there will be 22 flipchart papers (Note: You may decide to use fewer statements and/or to add some that are particularly relevant for your team.)

A marker for each member

STEPS

1. Ask members to complete the Team Culture Audit individually. Allow 10 minutes for individual work.

2. Following their individual work, ask members to wander around the room, recording their responses on the wall charts for each of the statements listed on the Team Culture Audit.

3. After members have recorded their responses, ask members to wander around and review the flipcharts. Ask members to choose several issues that are important for them to discuss. Often, these will be flipcharts where there is disagreement among the members.

4. Ask the members to discuss and to create helpful group norms for behaviors they wish to encourage.

5. This exercise can be repeated periodically to help the team work through their expectations for good team behavior.

Team Culture Audit

Which of the following do you think are good team behaviors?

1. I believe it is okay to discuss group business outside of the team.

2. I believe team members should be allowed to be late, leave early, or miss meetings.

3. I believe the team workload should be distributed equally among team members.

4. I believe that team members should participate equally at team meetings.

5. I believe team members should be permitted to discuss their views vigorously.

6. I believe that it is okay to raise my voice and yell to get my point across.

7. I am comfortable with members displaying emotion (e.g., anger, frustration) at our meetings.

8. I believe joke-telling is appropriate at our meetings.

9. I believe that we should talk about our team taboos (we should put the monster on the table).

10. I believe that it is okay for some team members to form special relationships with each other.

11. I believe it is okay to discuss team issues or agenda items in subgroups before team meetings.

12. Lobbying, so to speak, is permitted.

13. I believe we should get to know each other on a deep personal level and that we should spend time at team meetings fostering our relationships.

14. I believe that we should have a formal team leader.

15. I believe that our team leader should be our supervisor.

16. I believe the leadership role should be rotated and shared.

17. I believe that we should make most decisions by consensus.

18. I believe we should use a formal process for problem solving.

19. I believe we should be able to give each other and receive constructive criticism.

20. I believe that we need to support each other when dealing with other teams and our supervisors.

21. I believe that if our team is experiencing difficulty, we should go to management or HR for help.

22. I believe it is important to regularly review our functioning at team meetings.

EXERCISE 2.10: BLIND TRUST WALK

OBJECTIVES

To help members understand how important trust is as a foundation for effective team management practices.

TIME REQUIRED

1 hour +

BACKGROUND

See Chapter 2, "Creating Smart Team Management Practices."

MATERIALS REQUIRED

One blindfold for every two-person pairing

A path, preferably outdoors, with obstacles for the pair to walk through; a playground is the perfect setting

STEPS

1. Divide the team in half and blindfold half of the members.

2. Instruct the team that their task is to get everyone through the course. (You will have established the course prior to the beginning of the exercise.)

3. Explain to the pairings that they should take a few minutes to discuss some ground rules. For example, does the follower want to be "talked through" only, or would he or she prefer to also be "led physically"?

4. Ask the team to follow you as you negotiate the obstacles so that you can ensure a consistent level of challenge. After 10 minutes, switch roles and repeat the process.

5. Observe the group closely to watch for behaviors that helped and hindered their success.

6. Debrief the exercise by asking some of the following questions, or create your own:
   - ❖ Were you more comfortable leading or being led? Why?
   - ❖ As a leader, how did you communicate trustworthiness? What did you learn about leadership?
   - ❖ As a follower, did you get the support and direction you needed? How? If not, why not? What did you learn about being a follower?
   - ❖ How do you know how much support to give others on the team?

❖ What is it that makes you trust someone? What does trust look like?

❖ What did you learn about yourself in this exercise that will help you become a more effective team member?

7. What lessons can we apply to our own team functioning?

Note: If the group is large, several facilitators will be necessary, both to demonstrate to the "seeing" member what the "blind" member must do and to make sure that no accidents happen.

CHAPTER 3
EXERCISE 3.1: TEAM PROBLEM-SOLVING ASSESSMENT

OBJECTIVES

To assess the strength of your team's problem-solving skills.

To identify helpful processes your team needs to put in place to enhance the way you problem-solve.

TIME REQUIRED

1 hour to complete assessment and discuss

BACKGROUND

See Chapter 3, "Team Problem Solving for Pros."
This assessment can be used periodically with your team to assess the development and use of effective problem-solving techniques.

MATERIALS REQUIRED

Copies of the Team Problem-Solving Assessment for each member

STEPS

1. Distribute copies of the Team Problem-Solving Assessment to each member.

2. Ask each member to complete the assessment individually. Explain that the instruments will be reviewed collectively to show the team's combined assessment.

3. Share the range of responses for each question. Ask participants to discuss why they answered the way they did, particularly where most members scored the question low.

4. Identify the problem-solving techniques that need improvement. Discuss ways to improve each area requiring work.

5. **Discussion Question**: What processes can we put in place to enhance each area that was identified as needing improvement?

Team Problem-Solving Assessment

Use the following checklist to assess whether your team is using good problem-solving techniques and skills. Use the scale provided to rate the team *as a whole, on average.* Use the space below the scale to make finer observations.

Synergy

1. To what extent does the team build on each other's ideas?

1	2	3	4	5
Completely, all the time	Most of the time	Sometimes yes Sometimes no	Not very often	Not at all

2. The team's solution surpasses what any member could do alone.

1	2	3	4	5
Completely, all the time	Most of the time	Sometimes yes Sometimes no	Not very often	Not at all

3. The team puts together ideas in a way that no one in the group could do alone.

1	2	3	4	5
Completely, all the time	Most of the time	Sometimes yes Sometimes no	Not very often	Not at all

4. When developing a solution, the team does more than simply combine the various members' perspectives.

1	2	3	4	5
Completely, all the time	Most of the time	Sometimes yes Sometimes no	Not very often	Not at all

Communications Patience

5. The team makes sure it listens to each member and solicits ideas from quiet members.

1	2	3	4	5
Completely, all the time	Most of the time	Sometimes yes Sometimes no	Not very often	Not at all

6. The team takes action to prevent any individual member or subgroup of members from dominating the discussion.

1	2	3	4	5
Completely, all the time	Most of the time	Sometimes yes Sometimes no	Not very often	Not at all

7. Members of the team try hard to understand other members' points of view.

1	2	3	4	5
Completely, all the time	Most of the time	Sometimes yes Sometimes no	Not very often	Not at all

8. When a member has difficulty making himself or herself understood, that team member demonstrates patience and tries to formulate his or her thoughts in a clearer manner.

1	2	3	4	5
Completely, all the time	Most of the time	Sometimes yes Sometimes no	Not very often	Not at all

9. When a member has difficulty making himself or herself understood, the other team members are patient and allow that member to reformulate his or her thoughts in a clearer manner.

1	2	3	4	5
Completely, all the time	Most of the time	Sometimes yes Sometimes no	Not very often	Not at all

10. The team seems to sense or realize what others are trying to say. In other words, the team has developed an intuitive understanding of each other's meanings.

1	2	3	4	5
Completely, all the time	Most of the time	Sometimes yes Sometimes no	Not very often	Not at all

11. Members do not suppress their ideas or the ideas of others.

1	2	3	4	5
Completely, all the time	Most of the time	Sometimes yes Sometimes no	Not very often	Not at all

12. Team members feel free to express their dissenting ideas and thoughts without fear of offending others.

1	2	3	4	5
Completely, all the time	Most of the time	Sometimes yes Sometimes no	Not very often	Not at all

Problem-Solving Process

13. The team challenges and critically evaluates all proposals and solutions.

1	2	3	4	5
Completely, all the time	Most of the time	Sometimes yes Sometimes no	Not very often	Not at all

14. The team has agreed upon an effective method or strategy for making decisions and follows it.

1	2	3	4	5
Completely, all the time	Most of the time	Sometimes yes Sometimes no	Not very often	Not at all

EXERCISE 3.2: THE FIVE WS (WHO, WHAT, WHEN, WHERE, WHY)

OBJECTIVES

To help members collect relevant data about the problem they are facing. Use *who, what, when, where,* and *why* questions to collect relevant information about your problem's scope, causes, and effects. The possibilities and variations of these five questions are numerous. We will offer a few examples.

TIME REQUIRED

Varies depending on team problem to be solved

BACKGROUND

See Chapter 3, "Team Problem Solving for Pros."

MATERIALS REQUIRED

Flipchart paper and markers

STEPS

1. Ask participants to brainstorm the answers to the following questions concerning your problem. More than likely, team members will need to schedule interviews with stakeholders and other experts to discover the answer to many of these questions firsthand.

Who

Who is causing the problem?

Who is affected by the problem?

Who is this issue a problem for? Who is most impacted by the problem?

Who has done something about it?

Who else has solved this problem?

What

What is not working? What is going wrong?

What are the symptoms?

What are the consequences for others?

What is being done to address this problem right now? Is it working?

When

When is the problem occurring?

When is the problem not occurring?

When did it begin occurring?

Where

Where is the problem occurring?

Why

By asking "why?" five times, you increase the likelihood of cutting through the symptoms of a problem and arriving at its root cause.

Why did this problem occur?

Why are the errors occurring?

How

How did this problem start?

How are we responding to this problem?

How are our customers reacting to this problem?

How have others with similar problems solved this issue?

EXERCISE 3.3: IS/IS NOT

OBJECTIVES

To help members collect relevant data about what's working and what's not working with respect to a particular problem. Sometimes, knowing what works is just as important as knowing what is not working when crafting a problem statement and generating options for solutions.

TIME REQUIRED

Varies depending on team problem to be solved

BACKGROUND

See Chapter 3, "Team Problem Solving for Pros."

MATERIALS REQUIRED

Flipchart paper and markers

STEPS

1. Create a flipchart with the two poles of relevant questions, such as those listed below:

The issue or problem	
What is working?	What is not working?
Who is affected?	Who is not affected?
When is it occurring?	When is it not occurring?

2. Brainstorm the answers to both poles of the questions.

3. When in doubt of the answers, interview key stakeholders and customers to obtain firsthand data.

EXERCISE 3.4: FORCE FIELD ANALYSIS

OBJECTIVES

To help members collect relevant data about all of the forces (positive and negative) that are influencing a particular issue, problem, or solution.

TIME REQUIRED

Varies depending on team problem to be solved

BACKGROUND

See Chapter 3, "Team Problem Solving for Pros."

MATERIALS REQUIRED

Flipchart paper and markers

STEPS

1. Create a flipchart, clearly stating the problem or issue to be discussed. For example, "What prevents this organization from reducing scrap?" or "What prevents this team from delivering our product on time, every time?"

2. Next, ask members to brainstorm all of the forces in the organization contributing to the problem. Then, ask members to brainstorm all of the forces helping members to solve the problem.

The issue or problem
(Scrap costs through the roof)

Forces Contributing	Forces Helping
List all the things happening right now that are contributing to the scrap problem.	List all the things happening right now that are helping to reduce our scrap problem.

3. When in doubt of the answers, interview key stakeholders and customers to obtain firsthand data.

4. Discuss the information and its relative impact and determine what additional data, if any, should be collected to understand the problem and its causes more fully.

*Assessing Solutions: Force field analysis can also be used to assess solutions and create action plans. Simply replace the problem statement with a solution statement and assess the forces moving the organization toward the solution and then the forces blocking the organization from moving forward. Next, brainstorm all the ideas you have for "moving the needle" toward the proposed solution. These ideas will form your action plans.

Exercise 3.5: Hearing From our Stakeholders

OBJECTIVES

To understand the problem or issue from your stakeholders' points of view. Stakeholders can share critical information respecting problem analysis, important trends, and customer expectations.

TIME REQUIRED

Varies depending on team problem to be solved

BACKGROUND

See Chapter 3, "Team Problem Solving for Pros." This exercise was adapted from the work of Kathie Dannemiller, who uses a similar process in her Real-Time Strategic Change Meetings.

MATERIALS REQUIRED

Flipchart paper and markers

STEPS

1. First, identify who (which stakeholders) should be consulted. What key information and perspectives are you missing that will help your team understand the problem and its potential solutions more fully? Create a list of the information you require.

2. In advance of the meeting, brief the stakeholder(s) on your team problem and present them with your list of questions.

3. Ask each stakeholder to present his or her information. Following the presentation, give your team 15 minutes or so to discuss the following: What did we hear? What are our reactions? What questions of understanding do we have?

4. Share your thoughts and reactions with each stakeholder. Ask the stakeholder to answer your questions.

* Most stakeholders will be delighted to help your team. In the past, the teams we have worked with have collected meaningful information and perspectives from many kinds of stakeholders, including the following:

❖ CEO—providing critical information on the organization's major challenges, opportunities, strengths, and weaknesses

❖ CFO—providing critical information on key financial metrics and major cost factors

❖ Customers—providing key information on what your team needs to do to remain or become competitive

❖ Industry trends experts—providing key information on major trends impacting your team such as customer expectations, technological advances, new competitive entrants, supplier strategies, and so on

❖ Suppliers—providing key information on pricing strategies, quality standards, logistics systems, and so on

❖ Subject matter experts—providing key expertise to help you identify problems and generate solutions

EXERCISE 3.6: CAUSE-AND-EFFECT ANALYSIS

OBJECTIVES

To collect data about your team members' perceptions of the root causes of a particular problem. We typically use the traditional cause categories of *people*, *policies*, *procedures*, and *resources*. Your team should select whatever "cause categories" make sense to you.

TIME REQUIRED

1 hour +

BACKGROUND

See Chapter 3, "Team Problem Solving for Pros."

MATERIALS REQUIRED

Flipchart paper with the cause-and-effect diagram attached

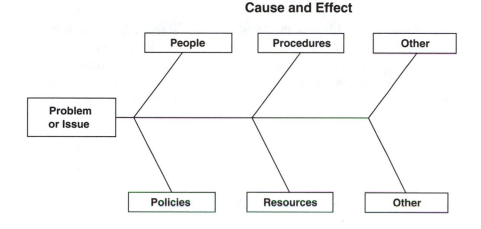

Cause and Effect

Markers
Post-it notes (if using)

STEPS

1. Select a problem or issue that you want to assess. Write it in the appropriate box.

2. Next, select the cause categories and ask team members to brainstorm all the possible causes of the problem, writing each cause in the appropriate cause category.

3. As you collect each possible cause, ask members *why* to generate a deeper understanding of the root cause, as opposed to symptoms.

4. Test your team's thinking by sharing the cause-and-effect diagram with key stakeholders. The more perspectives and data you collect, the more likely you are to uncover the real root causes.

ADAPTATIONS

❖ You may ask the team to multivote on the causes they believe are the most significant for further study.

❖ Ask the participants to individually write their causes on Post-it notes and then to place the notes in the appropriate cause category.

EXERCISE 3.7: CRAFTING A PROBLEM STATEMENT

OBJECTIVES

To define the problem so that your team can start working on the most pressing issues. Now that you have collected your data, you need to synthesize it and use it to craft a problem statement. This process may be quite simple; sometimes the problem statement simply emerges from your analysis. It might take some time to get the statement just right. In this exercise, we offer some tips.

TIME REQUIRED

Varies depending on team problem to be solved

BACKGROUND

See Chapter 3, "Team Problem Solving for Pros."

MATERIALS REQUIRED

Flipchart paper and markers

STEPS

Option: The Real Problem Is . . .

As you gather data and perspectives from various stakeholders and experts, continue to refine your problem definition. With each new definition, the problem will become clearer. Defining the problem three or four times is not uncommon. Keep each iteration of the problem to show your team how the problem definition has evolved over time.

Option: State the Problem As a Question

A problem definition works well if it is stated as a question, because a question invites an answer. So instead of "To create a marketing plan to sell more widgets," try "How do we sell more widgets?" Instead of "To reduce scrap," try "How can we reduce scrap?"

Option: Separate the Issues Into Mini-Problems

Depending on your problem's scope and complexity, you will find that there are several mini-problems that can be tackled more efficiently separately. Keeping them separate may make them easier to define and solve. Once a number of issues have been identified, ask your members to "multivote" on the highest-priority issues for resolution. The highest-priority issues for resolution can be determined via a number of questions, such as the following:

- ❖ What is the most urgent issue for resolution?
  - Which issue will give us the greatest impact?
  - Which issue, if tackled first, will help resolve the other issues?
  - Which issue will have the greatest payoff?
- ❖ Which issue are we motivated to tackle first?

Multivoting is a quick and efficient tool for helping the team sort and prioritize ideas for consideration. After a list of ideas has been generated, usually via brainstorming, members vote with their feet, as they are each given five to seven dots or check marks to place beside the ideas they prefer. The ideas receiving the most votes are circled. The process is repeated until the group has identified a workable number of items. The great value of this tool is that it helps the group focus discussion on the ideas that are the most important to the group.

EXERCISE 3.8: LIVING IN ANOTHER PERSON'S WORLD

OBJECTIVES

To help members develop good listening skills.

TIME REQUIRED

30 minutes

BACKGROUND

See Chapter 3, "Team Problem Solving for Pros."

MATERIALS REQUIRED

Copies of the Living in Another Person's World form for each member

STEPS

1. Distribute the Living in Another Person's World form to each member.

2. Ask members to select a topic that they have strong feelings about—this topic needs to be something that they are willing to share with another person—and to write down two or three sentences describing the topic, how they feel about it, and why they feel the way they do.

3. Ask members to work in pairs, with one person taking on the role of the speaker and the other assuming the role of the listener. Explain that the speaker tells the listener her opinion in about 2–3 minutes. The listener listens for understanding and, when appropriate, acknowledges the speaker by paraphrasing her statements and feeding back her feelings about the issue. The listener must do this to the speaker's satisfaction. If he does not, the speaker will say "not quite" and will repeat her point. The listener should acknowledge and paraphrase at least two times.

4. Ask members to switch roles and repeat.

5. Ask members to reflect on their experiences as listener and speaker:
   ❖ How did it feel?
   ❖ What might you do differently?
   ❖ What did you learn about the listening process?

Living in Another Person's World

To develop your listening skills as a patient communicator, try this exercise with a close friend or another team member. We've also found these skills to be very helpful when communicating with a spouse, especially in an emotionally driven moment. We call this exercise "Living in Another

Person's World" because the challenge is to truly understand the speaker from their frame of reference, or their world, before you reply.

1. Think about a topic that you have strong feelings about. This topic needs to be something that you are willing to share with another person. Write down two or three sentences describing the topic, how you feel about it, and why you feel the way you do. Some topic examples include your views on a law such as gun control or your government's performance over the past year.

2. Working in pairs, the speaker tells the listener her opinion in about 2–3 minutes. The listener listens for understanding and, when appropriate, acknowledges the speaker by paraphrasing her statements and feeding back her feelings about the issue. The listener must do this to the speaker's satisfaction. If he does not, the speaker will say "not quite" and will repeat her point. The listener should acknowledge and paraphrase at least two times.

3. Switch roles and repeat.

4. Reflect on your experiences as listener and speaker:
   ❖ How did it feel?
   ❖ What might you do differently?
   ❖ What did you learn about the listening process?

EXERCISE 3.9: WHO'S ON FIRST?

OBJECTIVES

To help members develop the communications patience skills of listening for understanding and speaking for understanding.

TIME REQUIRED

30 minutes

BACKGROUND

See Chapter 3, "Team Problem Solving for Pros."

MATERIALS REQUIRED

Audiotape of Abbott & Costello's recording "Who's on First"

STEPS

1. Ask members to listen to the famous recording of Abbott & Costello, "Who's on First." The recording is 5 minutes long, and we suggest that you play at least 2–3 minutes of it.

2. Following the recording, ask members to reflect on the factors that blocked effective communications. Common responses include the following:
   ❖ They were listening from different points of view.
   ❖ They made different assumptions.
   ❖ They did not listen for understanding.
   ❖ They did not take the time to explain fully.

3. Ask members to identify lessons from this discussion that we can apply to our team problem solving.

4. Recap points made and translate them into specific commitments for action.

TRAINING ADAPTATION

This exercise can be used in a training setting to introduce the concept of communications patience. Do the exercise and then follow with a short lecture on the elements of communications patience.

EXERCISE 3.10: CONCEPT CHALLENGE

OBJECTIVES

To help team members bust their assumptions about the way things are or should be.

TIME REQUIRED

Approximately 30 minutes (time varies with the topic)

BACKGROUND

See Chapter 3, "Team Problem Solving for Pros."

MATERIALS REQUIRED

Flipcharts and markers

STEPS

1. Select a topic or concept to be challenged. For example, a conference-planning team may select the concept that "training should not occur on weekends," a quality team may select a concept such as "only supervisors have the authority to stop the assembly line," and a restaurant may test the concept that "allowing smoking increases business."

2. Ask participants to reflect on the following:
    ❖ Why must we do it this way? Collect responses. With each answer, again ask why.
    ❖ What other alternatives may there be? Collect responses.

From your new data, ask participants to identify what new processes, procedures, or ways of thinking they would like to put in place.

TRAINING ADAPTATION

The following are concepts that we tend to challenge in the classroom:
❖ Marriage

❖ The standard 40-hour-per-week work schedule

❖ The schooling years are from age 5 to age 25

EXERCISE 3.11: CONSIDER ALL FACTORS

OBJECTIVES

To help team members examine all the factors that contribute to a particular idea, option, or solution.

To help team members evaluate the feasibility of a particular idea, option, or solution.

TIME REQUIRED

Approximately 30 minutes (time varies with the topic)

BACKGROUND

See Chapter 3, "Team Problem Solving for Pros."

MATERIALS REQUIRED

Flipcharts and markers

STEPS

1. Select a topic or scenario to be examined.

2. Ask participants to then search for all the factors involved in a situation. Explain that you will collect and record their responses using the brainstorming rules so that all responses are valid and should not be criticized. (Refer to the brainstorming guidelines on page 163.)

3. Create a mind map of their responses as they call them out.

4. Once participants have identified all the factors, ask them to discuss the following:
    ❖ How the idea or option could be altered or improved
    ❖ Whether they still believe the idea is a good one

TRAINING ADAPTATION

Topics or scenarios we examine in the classroom include the following:

1. You are a committee appointed by the government to assess the plausibility of introducing a new breakfast pill on the market. If people take one pill in the morning at breakfast time, they will not need to eat again until dinner. What are all the factors associated with introducing this new pill?

2. You are members of city council, considering whether or not to ban squeegee kids from the downtown core. What are all the factors associated with this decision?

Exercise 3.12: Brainstorming

OBJECTIVES

To help team members generate as many ideas as possible for a particular topic or scenario. The group should strive for quantity, not quality.

> *brain•storm* 1. A sudden and violent disturbance in the brain   2. A sudden, clever, whimsical, or foolish idea

TIME REQUIRED

Approximately 30 minutes (time varies with the topic)

BACKGROUND

See Chapter 3, "Team Problem Solving for Pros."

Brainstorming works because it is a structured process of wild thinking followed by a thorough evaluation of the ideas. The best thinking comes when you follow the guidelines.

Always use a flipchart to display ideas so that everyone can see them. This stimulates thinking. As flipchart pages are filled, post them on the wall so that the group can continue to see them.

MATERIALS REQUIRED

Flipcharts and markers

STEPS

1. Clarify the topic or issue for brainstorming and write it on the top of a flipchart.

2. Review the following rules:
   - ❖ Do not evaluate or judge the ideas that members generate.
   - ❖ Offer your wild ideas: Do not evaluate or edit your own thoughts before offering.
   - ❖ Everyone is encouraged, but not pressured, to participate.
   - ❖ Build on and combine ideas already generated.

3. Be sure to encourage free thinking. The benefit of wild ideas is that they often stimulate a new thought. They are also sometimes humorous, and humor seems to be one of the ingredients for creative thinking. Remember, if the leader does not offer a wild idea, chances are no one else will.

4. Record all ideas on a flipchart so that everyone can see them. Make sure you record the idea as stated; do not censor ideas or write them in your own words. Once all ideas are out, review and evaluate them. Lead a discussion to clarify and combine like ideas if appropriate.

5. Evaluate and code each suggestion according to its feasibility, usefulness, and impact.

EXERCISE 3.13:
BRAINSTORMING PRACTICE WITH AN EXAMPLE

OBJECTIVES

To practice the process of brainstorming with a silly example. This exercise is particularly useful if you are teaching the concept.

TIME REQUIRED

Approximately 30 minutes (time varies with the topic)

BACKGROUND

See Chapter 3, "Team Problem Solving for Pros."

MATERIALS REQUIRED

Flipcharts and markers

STEPS

1. Say, "Assume you are a bathroom designer extraordinaire. Your client has asked you to develop the bathtub of all bathtubs. Brainstorm as many bathtub innovations as you can in a 10-minute period."
   "Ways to improve the bathtub . . . "

2. Review the following rules:
   ❖ Do not evaluate or judge the ideas that members generate.
   ❖ Offer your wild ideas: Do not evaluate or edit your own thoughts before offering.

> ❖ Everyone is encouraged, but not pressured, to participate.
> ❖ Build on and combine ideas already generated.

3. Be sure to encourage free thinking. The benefit of wild ideas is that they often stimulate a new thought.

4. Record all ideas on a flipchart so that everyone can see them. This will stimulate thinking. As flipchart pages are filled, post them on the wall so that the group can continue to see them.

5. Once all ideas are out, review and evaluate them. Lead a discussion to clarify and combine like ideas if appropriate.

6. Evaluate and code each suggestion according to its feasibility, usefulness, and impact.

EXERCISE 3.14: EXPLORING ASSUMPTIONS

OBJECTIVES

To give members practice surfacing and exploring assumptions.

This exercise can also be used to explore assumptions held by members with live team issues; simply substitute your own team topic for the experts'.

TIME REQUIRED

Approximately 30 minutes (time varies with the topic)

BACKGROUND

See Chapter 3, "Team Problem Solving for Pros."

MATERIALS REQUIRED

Select excerpt: "Senator Mischief" or "What to Do About John?"

Copies of the Exploring Assumptions Checklist for each member

STEPS

1. Provide copies of the excerpt and the Exploring Assumptions Checklist to each member; allow 5 minutes for personal reading time. (If you are working with a live issue, clarify the issue for discussion.)

2. Ask members to discuss the issue, answering the following questions:
   ❖ What is the problem?
   ❖ How should the problem be solved?

3. After 10–15 minutes of discussion, stop the discussion to reflect on the following:
   ❖ Have we surfaced our assumptions? Have we explored our assumptions?
   ❖ How do our assumptions differ? How are they the same?
   ❖ How can we come to an agreement?

4. Ask, "What lessons from this discussion can we apply to our team problem solving?"

5. Recap points made and translate them into specific commitments for action.

The Exploring Assumptions Checklist

Keep this checklist of questions available to use as needed to help surface assumptions and aid understanding:

Ask members to explore their assumptions for reality.

❖ What information are you basing that on? What evidence do you have? What facts do you have to confirm that?

❖ What are the assumptions that must be true in order for this solution to work?

Ask members to share how they interpret a scenario.

❖ If we do x, is y likely to occur? What are all the assumptions that must be true for y to occur?

Test assumptions held by the group.

❖ What assumptions are evident in the decisions we have made so far?

❖ Are they still valid? How have they changed?

❖ How have these assumptions limited us?

**Ask members to share the
reasons why they feel the way they do.**

❖ What's your opinion of *x*?

❖ Do you think it will work? Why or why not?

❖ How do you think people will react if we do *x*? Why?

❖ What are your concerns?

Ask members to share what's important to them.

❖ If our plan were a huge success, what outcomes would we achieve?

❖ Why is this solution important to you?

❖ What criteria must we meet to achieve a solution that we can all live with?

Individually read the following excerpt.

Senator Mischief

OTTAWA – The chronically truant Senator Andrew Thompson will be stripped of his office, secretary, telephone and most travel privileges until he begins showing up for work on Parliament Hill.

The Senate voted last night to adopt the report of its internal economy committee, which concluded last week that sanctions must be applied against the Liberal senator from Ontario, who has attended less than 3 per cent of the chamber's sittings since 1990. . . .

The truancy of their colleague drew Canada's senators in recent days into extended navel gazing. What began as a debate on whether to discipline the wayward Mr. Thompson, who has been to work just 14 times this decade, expanded in recent days to a much broader discussion of whether substantive reform is needed to repair the image of the chamber of "sober second thought."

Should a senator's claimed illness need to be confirmed? Should a member be credited with attendance if he or she shows up for only five minutes? What sort of public business should a senator be able to pursue without being fined for absence?

(Continued)

(Continued)

Some senators have called for a strict code of conduct that would punish those who fail to show up for the bulk of the roughly 70 Senate sittings each year. . . . At the same time, a backlash has started to develop among some who feel their colleagues are succumbing to unreasonable pressure from the media and the public. . . .

"What troubles me is that, somehow, the media has established attendance in this chamber as the No. 1 measure of the legitimacy of this place and those who serve in it," Conservative William Kelly said Monday to cheers from many of his peers. "I do not think that we should accept that standard or succumb to the assumptions that underlie it."

SOURCE: Eisenhardt, K., 2000, August 7. Reprinted with permission of *The Globe and Mail.*

After you have read the article, do the following:

1. Discuss and come to agreement on the following points:
   ❖ What the problem is
   ❖ How you would solve this problem

2. Reflect on your assumptions. How did you explore them? How did you reach agreement?

Individually read the following excerpt.

What to Do About John?

John is a good student. The eldest of five children, at the age of 18 he is a responsible, hardworking young man who excels in school despite working 20 hours per week at the corner store.

No one was more excited than John was when he learned that he was the recipient of the Wood Scholarship for the Kingston School of Science and Technology. Securing this scholarship meant that John could acquire a world-class education in science and technology, and if he did well, he would receive funding to any university he wished to attend in North America. John had always dreamed of going to Queen's University.

Three months into the program, John was sitting in the director's office awaiting his fate. Although John was doing well academically, he was not doing well socially. In fact, several senior students had taken a disliking to John, openly bullying him and making rude remarks about him in front of others.

John did not report his problems to administration. In hindsight, he wished that he had. Just yesterday, the seniors came up to him in the cafeteria and dumped his plate of spaghetti over his head. John was publicly humiliated. He took what remained of his dinner and threw it at one of his perpetrators. In an instant, a food fight erupted.

The director has asked you to advise her on how to deal with John and the other boys. The policy, which everyone knows and understands, specifically forbids fighting of any kind and specifies that the punishment for fighting is expulsion.

1. Come to a group consensus on how you will solve this problem.

2. Reflect on your assumptions. How did you explore them? How did you reach agreement?

EXERCISE 3.15: CONSEQUENCES AND SEQUELS

OBJECTIVES

To help members evaluate an idea before it is discounted.

To help members examine decisions before they are made.

By thinking through and responding to the various implications of our decisions, we develop solutions that work and that members can commit to.

TIME REQUIRED

Approximately 1 hour (time varies with the topic)

BACKGROUND

See Chapter 3, "Team Problem Solving for Pros."

MATERIALS REQUIRED

Flipchart and markers

STEPS

1. Ask members to assess the immediate, short-term, and long-term consequences of a problem, a decision, or an event.

2. Define the time range for each category. For example, *immediate* might be today, *short term* may be up to one month, and *long term* may be up to six months. The time ranges will vary with the topic of your analysis.

3. Ask members to brainstorm each list (immediate, short term, and long term) one at a time, allowing about 10 minutes for each list.

4. Before brainstorming, review and apply the rules of brainstorming as follows:
   ❖ Do not evaluate or judge the ideas that members generate.
   ❖ Offer your wild ideas: Do not evaluate or edit your own thoughts before offering.
   ❖ Everyone is encouraged, but not pressured, to participate.
   ❖ Build on and combine ideas already generated.

5. Record all ideas on a flipchart so that everyone can see them. This will stimulate thinking. As flipchart pages are filled, post them on the wall so that the group can continue to see them.

6. Once the team has completed their lists, review and discuss.

7. Ask the group to next reflect on the question "So what?" or "What are the implications for our decision?"

TRAINING ADAPTATION

If you are using this exercise in the training classroom, you can work with a live team issue. If you are using it for practice, select a wild and crazy idea for your team to explore, such as the introduction of new technology (e.g., a personal lie detector, a personal monitoring system, or phones with cameras so you can see the caller).

EXERCISE 3.16: PLUSES, MINUSES, SO WHAT?

OBJECTIVES

To analyze the feasibility of a decision.

To help members fully examine ideas before they are discounted.

To help members test decisions before they are made.

By thinking through and responding to the various implications of our decisions, we develop solutions that work and that members can commit to.

TIME REQUIRED

Approximately 1 hour (time varies with the topic)

BACKGROUND

See Chapter 3, "Team Problem Solving for Pros."

MATERIALS REQUIRED

Flipchart and markers

STEPS

1. Ask members to identify the pluses and minuses of a possible scenario, idea, or option under consideration.

2. Ask members to brainstorm each list (pluses/minuses) one at a time, allowing at least 10 minutes for each list.

3. Before brainstorming, review and apply the rules of brainstorming as follows:
   ❖ Do not evaluate or judge the ideas that members generate.
   ❖ Offer your wild ideas: Do not evaluate or edit your own thoughts before offering.
   ❖ Everyone is encouraged, but not pressured, to participate.
   ❖ Build on and combine ideas already generated.

4. Record all ideas on a flipchart so that everyone can see them. This will stimulate thinking. As flipchart pages are filled, post them on the wall so that the group can continue to see them.

5. Once the team has completed their lists, review and discuss.

6. Ask the group to next reflect on the question "So what?" or "How can we adapt our decision to accommodate the pluses and minimize the minuses?"

TRAINING ADAPTATION

If you are using this exercise in the training classroom, you can work with a live team issue. If you are using it for practice, select a wild and crazy idea for your team to explore, such as the introduction of new technology (e.g., a personal lie detector, a personal monitoring system, or a phone with a camera so you can see the caller).

EXERCISE 3.17: BLIND SQUARE

OBJECTIVES

This exercise can be used to highlight all the problem-solving skills including listening for understanding; speaking for understanding; challenging assumptions; building on ideas; being willing to follow as well as lead; being willing to risk being wrong; being assertive, not aggressive; and using a problem-solving process.

TIME REQUIRED

1 hour +

BACKGROUND

See Chapter 3, "Team Problem Solving for Pros."

MATERIALS REQUIRED

Blindfolds for each participant

A long rope, 20–40 feet long (the longer the rope, the harder the exercise)

A large clear space, preferably outdoors

STEPS

1. Ask members to stand in a circle, facing center, one arm's length apart. Ask them to blindfold themselves (check to make sure that no one is peeking).

2. Coil the rope at their feet (three coils).

3. Give consecutive members sections of the rope from different coils.

4. Explain as follows:

   "Your task is to create a perfect square. A perfect square has four sides of equal length, and each of the four corners is a 90-degree angle. You may not let go of the rope. You may move along it only as far as the next person, but you may not pass another person on the rope. You may not coil the rope. The task is done when the team says that it is done."

5. Observe the group closely to watch for behaviors that helped and hindered their success.

6. Debrief the exercise by asking some of the following questions, or create your own:
   - ❖ What did the team do well? What might you do differently next time?
   - ❖ Did you establish a problem-solving process? How did you establish it? Did you use it?
   - ❖ When and how did your problem-solving skills (listening for understanding, speaking for understanding, exploring assumptions, building on ideas, etc.) help you?
   - ❖ What did you learn about yourself in this exercise that will help you become a more effective team member?

Note: It is important during this exercise that the facilitators observe carefully to prevent accidents. Intervene if you think people are about to trip or otherwise hurt themselves. Intervene also if members are breaking the rules. If they take their hands off the rope, it will only tangle *more*, not less.

EXERCISE 3.18: GRID MAZE

OBJECTIVES

Problem Solving—This exercise can be used to highlight all the problem-solving skills including planning and using a problem-solving process; challenging assumptions; being willing to follow as well as lead; being willing to risk being wrong; being assertive, not aggressive; and being flexible as new data emerge.

Team Management Practices—This exercise is also very effective to reinforce good team management practices such as the importance of planning before acting, the importance of effective team norms for safety and inclusion, and the ability to trust oneself and others.

TIME REQUIRED

1 hour +

BACKGROUND

See Chapter 3, "Team Problem Solving for Pros."

MATERIALS REQUIRED

A grid maze (7 squares wide by 10 squares long. Squares should be 12 inches by 12 inches. The grid maze can be made from ropes, or you can use masking tape on the floor to create the image.)

A large, clear space, preferably outdoors

A copy of the grid maze rules

A horn or noisemaker

STEPS

1. Explain to members that before them lies the fearsome grid maze and then pass them the rules. Ensure that a member reads the rules out loud at least once.

2. Tell them that they can begin the task whenever they are ready. Emphasize that once a member steps onto the grid, nobody may speak until the exercise is over. Enforce this rule rigidly.

3. As the members negotiate their way through the grid maze, blow the horn (or use the noisemaker) when a member steps on a "bad" square. The member must then go back to the beginning of the maze using all "good" squares. If not, the next team member misses his or her turn. Don't betray any information by your expression or body language.

4. After two thirds of the group have passed through the maze, change the path. If they object, say, "Rules change, that's life." Do not demonstrate good leadership.

5. Observe the group closely to watch for behaviors that helped and hindered their success.

6. Debrief the exercise by asking some of the following questions, or create your own:
   - What did the team do well? What might you do differently next time?
   - Did you establish a plan? Did you use it?
   - Were you personally ready to start when the group did? If not, did you voice your concern? Why or why not?
   - How did you overcome the communications challenge posed by the silence rule? What did you learn about the communications process?
   - What talents and roles emerged? Did you use your resources fully? How did the roles change as members were on or outside of the grid?
   - What did failure sound like? Was it really the sound of failure, or was it simply helpful information?
   - How did you personally react to change?
   - What did you learn about yourself in this exercise that will help you become a more effective team member?

7. What behaviors and processes can we apply to our own team functioning?

The Grid Maze

Before you lies the fearsome grid maze. Your task is to get each member of your team through the maze to the other side.

Some of the spaces are "good" to stand on and some are not. If you stand on a "good" square, you will hear silence. If you stand on a "bad" square, you will hear a hideous squawking sound representing failure (ask for a demonstration!). Only the first row (seven squares) is available for your initial attempts.

Once you discover a good square, you may move to any adjacent square. You may move only to squares adjacent to the one you are standing on. Only one person at a time may be on the maze.

When you experience failure, your turn is over and you must leave the maze to recover your self-esteem and let the next member of your team have a try. When leaving the maze after a failure, you must follow the same pathway you used to enter it—that is, all the good squares. If, on the way out, you accidentally step on a known "bad" square, the next member of your team will miss his or her turn.

You may not take notes or mark the ground in any way.

One more thing: Once the first failure noise sounds, *nobody may talk again* until the whole team has passed through the maze.

Table 1   The Grid Maze

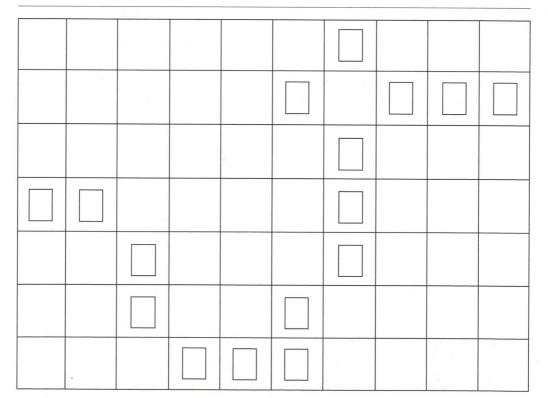

Table 2   The Grid Maze With Optional Changes

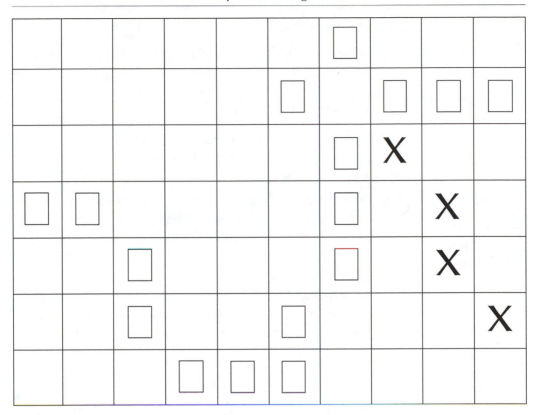

CHAPTER 4
EXERCISE 4.1: WIN ALL YOU CAN (X OR Y)

OBJECTIVES

To help members diagnose the many causes of conflict.

To understand one's conflict-handling style.

TIME REQUIRED

1 hour

BACKGROUND

See Chapter 4, "Handling Team Conflict."

MATERIALS REQUIRED

Copies of the Win All You Can exercise

(Optional) Copies of the Circle of Conflict exercise for each person

STEPS

1. Divide the group into three or four subgroups and ask each subgroup to go to a different corner of the room or have each group sit at a separate table.

2. Explain to members that they will be experiencing a situation that in many ways simulates the kinds of dilemmas we experience in the workplace.

3. Explain as follows:

   *"The objective of this exercise is to win all you can. For 10 successive rounds, you and your team are to choose an X or a Y. You will confer with your group during the time allowed and decide which to choose. When the signal is given, you will hold up your card with either the X or the Y on it **at the same time as the other groups**. You can earn money depending on the pattern of choices made in your groups."*

4. Show them the payoff schedule. We post it on a flipchart and leave it for all to see throughout the exercise. Also, read the rules out loud.

5. Give the subgroups 3–5 minutes to discuss their strategy before starting the game. Do not permit the subgroups to communicate with each other in any way. If they ask questions, do not answer them. You do not want to role-model good leadership.

6. Announce that the exercise in now beginning, and give the subgroups each 1½ minutes to make their first decision (they will choose to hold up either an X or a Y). After the 1½ minutes have elapsed, ask each team to hold up the card they selected (either an X or a Y). It is critical that they all hold their cards up at the same time. We usually say, "One, two, three, hold up your card."

7. On the basis of the cards they selected, score the first round as per the scoring matrix. Post this matrix so that everyone can see it. (It is helpful to have the matrix planned, prepared, and posted in advance. If you're not adept with fast arithmetic, have a helper calculate and write in the scores for you.)

8. Repeat the process for each round as per the time allotted on the scoring matrix. Record the scores for each round.

9. During rounds 5, 8, and 10, announce that each team can appoint a spokesperson to meet in the hall (or another private place) to discuss strategy. Allow a firm 2 minutes for these meetings.

10. Note also that during rounds 5, 8, and 10, the scoring is multiplied.

11. Following the last round, calculate the group scores. Teams will have adopted either a cooperative strategy, a competitive strategy, or a mix of both.

12. Debrief the exercise by discussing what strategies the team adopted (either cooperative, competitive, or both) and why.

DISCUSSION QUESTIONS

❖ What was your strategy?

❖ Did it work for you?

❖ What was it about the rules of this exercise that caused you to compete?

❖ What lessons can we apply to our team and workplace?

ADAPTATION

1. Review the causes of conflict with the group, as per the Circle of Conflict. Refer to Diagnosing the Key Causes of Conflict in Chapter 4, Handling Team Conflict, for your script.

2. Ask members to assess the causes of conflict from the standpoint of structure, values, relationships, data, and interests and to record in the space provided.

3. Discuss how the lessons learned can be applied to the causes of conflict in their workplace.

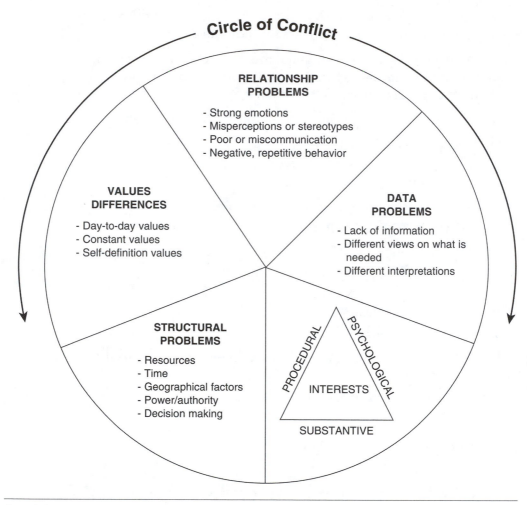

Circle of Conflict

RELATIONSHIP PROBLEMS
- Strong emotions
- Misperceptions or stereotypes
- Poor or miscommunication
- Negative, repetitive behavior

VALUES DIFFERENCES
- Day-to-day values
- Constant values
- Self-definition values

DATA PROBLEMS
- Lack of information
- Different views on what is needed
- Different interpretations

STRUCTURAL PROBLEMS
- Resources
- Time
- Geographical factors
- Power/authority
- Decision making

PROCEDURAL   PSYCHOLOGICAL
INTERESTS
SUBSTANTIVE

Win All You Can

The object of this exercise is to win all you can. It is played by three or four groups. For 10 successive rounds, you and your group are to choose an X or a Y. You will confer with your group during the time allowed and decide which to choose. When the signal is given, you will hold up your card with either the X or the Y on it *at the same time as the other groups.* You can earn money depending on the pattern of choices made by all groups as follows:

Four Groups		Three Groups	
4 Xs	Each group loses $1.	3 Xs	Each group loses $1.
3 Xs	Each group that chooses X wins $1.	2 Xs	Each group that chooses X wins $1.
1 Y	The group that chooses Y loses $3.	1 Y	The group that chooses Y loses $3.
2 Xs	Each group that chooses X wins $2.		
2 Ys	Each group that chooses Y loses $2.		
1 X	The group that chooses X wins $3.	1 X	The group that chooses X wins $3.
3 Ys	Each group that chooses Y loses $1.	2 Ys	Each group that chooses Y loses $1.
4 Ys	Each group wins $1.	3 Ys	Each group wins $1.

There are five rules:

1. You should write down your choice on the form provided as soon as your group agrees. Once it is written, it cannot be changed.

2. You may not talk to the other groups, except at times to be designated (see accompanying form).

3. You should keep a running total of your winnings and losses on the accompanying form.

4. Note that your payoff for bonus round 5 is multiplied by 3, bonus round 8 by 5, and bonus round 10 by 10.

5. In these three bonus rounds, a spokesperson from your group will be permitted to confer with the other groups' spokespersons prior to making a decision.

SOURCE: From Pfeiffer, J. W., & Jones, J. E., *Handbook of Structured Experiences for Human Relations Training, Vol. II.* Copyright © 1970. This material is used by permission of John Wiley & Sons, Inc.

Scoring Form

Each group should fill out this form for each round. Keep a running score of your winnings and losses, and calculate the final tally at the end of round 10.

Keep Track of the Decisions and Scores for Your Pair

Round	Time Allotted	Confer With	Choice: X or Y?	$ Won	$ Lost	Balance
1	**1½ min.**	Group				
2	1 min.	Group				
3	1 min.	Group				
4	1 min.	Group				
5	**2 min.**	**Spokespersons**				**x 3**
6	1 min.	Group				
7	1 min.	Group				
8	**2 min.**	**Spokespersons**				**x 5**
9	1 min.	Group				
10	**2 min.**	**Spokespersons**				**x 10**
					TOTAL:	

Exercise 4.2: Handling
Problems in Team Discussion Assessment

OBJECTIVES

To help members assess their approach to handling interpersonal behaviors as they occur.

TIME REQUIRED

1 hour

BACKGROUND

See Chapter 4, "Handling Team Conflict."

MATERIALS REQUIRED

Copies of the Handling Problems in Team Discussion instrument for each member

STEPS

1. Provide copies of the Handling Problems in Team Discussion instrument to each member. Allow 15 minutes for personal work. Explain that their assessments will be gathered and reviewed collectively to show the team's combined perspective.

2. As members complete the instrument, ask them to compute their score.

3. Collect individual scores and share the range of responses for each question. Ask participants to discuss why they answered the way they did, particularly where most members scored the question as "Yes" and "1" or "5."

4. Discuss ways to improve your conflict-handling ability.

DISCUSSION QUESTIONS

❖ What are the typical disruptive behaviors that occur in our group? Why are these behaviors disruptive?

❖ What processes can we put in place to enhance our ability to handle these conflicts and disruptive behaviors as they occur?

Handling Problems in Team Discussion

Here you will find descriptions of problems that sometimes happen in team discussions. There are different ways in which teams can handle each of these problems. It is important to know if your team has experienced any of these problems, and if it has, what your team did about the problem.

Think about how your team has worked together on various projects and tasks recently. Try to remember what happened in your most recent meetings. Read each sentence and decide whether or not it describes something that has happened in your team. If not, then circle *No* and continue to the next sentence.

If the sentence does describe something that has happened in your team, circle *Yes*. Then, read the descriptions of ways to handle these kinds of problems. Circle the number that best corresponds with how your team handled that problem.

Ways to Handle Problems

1. The group stopped discussion and openly acknowledged the problem. Solved the problem. Openly discussed and agreed on a procedure to deal with similar problems in the future.

2. The group stopped discussion and acknowledged the problem. Solved the problem through open discussion.

3. At least some group members acknowledged the problem. An attempt was made to solve it but was abandoned before the situation was corrected.

4. At least some group members acknowledged the problem. No attempt was made to correct the situation.

5. All members ignored the problem and continued discussion.

	Did this happen in your group? Circle one.	**If yes, circle description of group's behavior.** (See preceding descriptions.)				
		1	2	3	4	5
1. One group member talked out of turn.	No Yes	1	2	3	4	5
2. One group member didn't participate when expected to.	No Yes	1	2	3	4	5
3. One group member dominated the discussion too much.	No Yes	1	2	3	4	5
4. One group member spoke too loudly or forcefully.	No Yes	1	2	3	4	5
5. One group member was not open enough with her or his views.	No Yes	1	2	3	4	5
6. One group member did not listen enough.	No Yes	1	2	3	4	5
7. One group member assumed leadership in the discussion without other members agreeing to it.	No Yes	1	2	3	4	5
8. No one in the group knew how to proceed.	No Yes	1	2	3	4	5
9. Group members could not agree on how to proceed.	No Yes	1	2	3	4	5
10. One group member blocked discussion.	No Yes	1	2	3	4	5

11. One group member changed the topic before others were ready.	No	Yes	1	2	3	4	5
12. One group member kept going on about the same topic after others had finished it.	No	Yes	1	2	3	4	5
13. One group member discussed a topic no one else wanted to discuss.	No	Yes	1	2	3	4	5
14. Group members discussed things from different points of view.	No	Yes	1	2	3	4	5
15. One group member pushed his or her ideas on everyone else when it was not appropriate.	No	Yes	1	2	3	4	5
16. One group member disagreed with everyone else.	No	Yes	1	2	3	4	5
17. Group members could not agree on a decision.	No	Yes	1	2	3	4	5
18. At least one group member was confused or uncertain about the tasks.	No	Yes	1	2	3	4	5
TOTAL							

Scoring Your Responses

Step 1   Count the number of times you answered "Yes" to "Did this happen in your group?" The total number of "Yes" responses will be the Norms Violation Count. The higher this score, the more likely it is that your team will encounter "affective" conflict.
Count = _____

Step 2   Moving over to the next set of columns, add the circled 1s and place the total in the bottom. Do the same for the 2s, 3s, 4s, and 5s. Add all of these totals, which will be a number between 1 and 90. This is your team's Behavioral Response Score.
Behavioral Response Score = _____

Step 3   Divide the Behavioral Response Score by the Count. The resulting mean is an estimate of the skills with which your team handles problems in team discussions. The lower the score, the better.
Mean = _____

EXERCISE 4.3: CREATING HELPFUL NORMS AND PROTOCOLS

OBJECTIVES

To help your team identify the behaviors team members want to encourage and discourage.

To create norms and protocol for helping members work together effectively.

To develop a commitment to using them.

TIME REQUIRED

1 hour +

BACKGROUND

See Chapter 2, "Creating Smart Team Management Practices."

MATERIALS REQUIRED

Flipchart and markers

STEPS

1. Ask team members to reflect on the behaviors that will help the team function effectively. Record responses on a flipchart, under a heading labeled "Help."

2. Ask team members to reflect on behaviors that are hindering the team from achieving its objectives. Record responses on a flipchart labeled "Hinder."

Behaviors in the team that . . .	
Help	Hinder

Some Tips for Collecting Responses

1. Be sure to probe the team members for specific behaviors. For example, if participants suggest "showing respect for team members," probe the group for specific behaviors that show respect, such as "coming to meetings on time or listening for understanding."

2. Be sure to probe the team members for behaviors that will *help* or *hinder* all aspects of team functioning, including how the team solves problems, makes decisions, manages conflict, and manages its social processes (how included members feel) and task processes (how the work gets organized and accomplished). For example, if the group has not addressed decision making, ask, "What specific behaviors and processes will help or hinder us in making effective decisions?" If the group has not addressed communication, ask, "What specific behaviors can each team member do to ensure that we understand each other?"

3. After you have recorded all responses for helpful and hindering behaviors, ask members to place a dot or a check mark beside all of the behaviors they can commit to supporting.

4. From the remaining list of helpful and hindering behaviors, ask the group to create a "Thou Shall, Thou Shalt Not" list that incorporates all of the behaviors the team has agreed to do and not do.

5. Seek the team's permission to enforce the behaviors identified on the list. Explain that the facilitator, process observer, and all team members have the responsibility of ensuring that they are respected and used. Post the lists in the team meeting room.

VARIATIONS

We often encourage teams to develop their norms and protocols in three subsets: decision making, conflict handling, and social inclusion. This way, members focus on what is important to them in each subset and these important discussions do not get diluted.

References and Suggested Further Reading

Amabile, T. A. (1999). How to kill creativity. In *Harvard Business Review on breakthrough thinking*. Boston: Harvard Business Review Press.

Asch, S. (1953). Effects of group pressure upon the modification and distortion of judgements. In D. Cartwright & A. Zander (Eds.), *Group dynamics: Research and theory*. Evanston, IL: Row, Peterson and Company.

Beatty, C. (2002). Retrieved from http://www.industrialrelationscentre.com/publications/pdfs/research_academic_teams.pdf and http://www.industrialrelationscentre.com/publications/pdfs/high_performance.pdf

Beckhard, R. (1969). *Organization development: Strategies and models*. Reading, MA: Addison-Wesley.

Beckhard, R. (1972). *Organizational development*. Reading, MA: Addison-Wesley.

Beckhard, R. (1997). *Agent of change. My life, my practice*. San Francisco: Jossey-Bass.

Beckhard, R., & Harris, R. T. (1987). *Organizational transitions: Managing complex change* (2nd ed.). Don Mills, ON: Addison-Wesley.

Beckhard, R., & Pritchard, W. (1992). *Changing the essence*. San Francisco: Jossey-Bass.

Beer, M., & Nohria, N. (2000). *Breaking the code of change*. Boston: Harvard Business School Press.

Bell, E. C., & Blakeney, R. N. (1977). Personality correlates of conflict resolution modes. *Human Relations, 30*(9), 849–857.

Bergmann, T., & DeMeuse, K. (1996). Diagnosing whether an organization is truly ready to empower employees: A case study. *Journal of Human Resource Planning, 19*(1), 38–47.

Campion, M. A., Medsker, G. J., & Higgs, A. C. (1993). Relations between work-group characteristics and effectiveness: Implications for designing effective workgroups. *Personnel Psychology, 46*, 823–850.

Coser, L. (1956). *The functions of social conflict*. Glencoe, IL: Free Press.

Dannemiller Tyson Associates. (1994). *Real time strategic change: A consultant's guide to large-scale meetings*. Ann Arbor, MI: Author.

Dannemiller Tyson Associates. (2000). *Whole-scale change: Unleashing the magic in organizations.* San Francisco: Berrett-Koehler.

Dessler, G. (1980). *Organization theory: Integrating structure and behavior.* Englewood Cliffs, NJ: Prentice-Hall.

Deutsch, M. (1969). Conflicts: Productive and destructive. *Journal of Social Issues, 25*(1), 7–41.

Dyer, W. (1994). *Team building: Current issues and new alternatives* (3rd edition). Reading, MA: Addison-Wesley.

Eisenhardt, K. (2000, August 7). Senator mischief. *Globe & Mail.*

Festinger, L., Schachter, S., & Back, K. (1950). *Social pressures in informal groups: A study of a housing project.* New York: Harper & Row.

Fisher, K. (1993). *Leading self-directed work teams: A guide to developing new team leadership skills.* New York: McGraw Hill.

Fisher, R., & Ury, W. (1983). *Getting to yes: Negotiating agreement without giving in.* New York: Penguin Books.

Galtung, J. (1975). Is peaceful research possible? On the methodology of peaceful research. In *Peace research, education and action.* Copenhagen: Eilers.

Ghoshal, S., & Bartlett, C. (2000). *Breaking the code of change.* Boston: Harvard Business School Press.

Goleman, D. (1995). *Emotional intelligence.* New York: Bantam Books.

Goleman, D., Kaufmann, P., & Ray, M. (1992). *The creative spirit.* New York: Penguin.

Hackman, J. R. (1990). *Groups that work (and those that don't).* San Francisco: Jossey-Bass.

Hackman, J. R. (2002). *Leading teams: Setting the stage for great performances.* Boston: Harvard Business School Press.

Hackman, J. R., & Oldman, G. R. (1979). *Work redesign.* Reading, MA: Addison-Wesley.

Hall, J., & Watson, W. H. (1970). The effects of a normative intervention in group decision making performance. *Human Relations, 23,* 299–317.

Hammond, J., Keeney, R., & Raiffa, H. (1998). *Smart choices: A practical guide to making better decisions.* Boston: Harvard Business Review.

Hargadon, R., & Sutton, R. (2000, May/June). *Building an innovation factory.* Boston: Harvard Business.

Harrington-Mackin, D. (1994). *The team building tool kit: Tips, tactics and rules for effective workplace teams.* New York: American Management Association.

Harris, R. (2000, June). *Communicating change.* Presentation delivered at the Change Management: Mastering the Process Seminar, Queen's Industrial Relations Centre, Ontario.

Harvey, J. B. (1988). *The Abilene Paradox and other meditations on management.* San Francisco: Wiley.

Hellinghausen, M. A., & Myers, J. (1998, September/October). Empowered employees: A new team concept. *Industrial Management, 5,* 21–23.

Janis, I. L. (1971, November). Groupthink. *Psychology Today, 5*(6). (Reprinted in R. Steers & L. Porter, *Motivation and work behavior,* 3rd edition. New York: McGraw Hill.)

Janis, I. L. (1972). *Victims of groupthink.* Boston: Houghton Mifflin.

Kanter, R., Stein, B., & Jick, T. (1992). *Challenge of organizational change: How companies experience it and leaders guide it.* New York: New York Free Press.

Katzenbach, J. R. (1997). *Teams at the top: Unleashing the potential of both teams and individual leaders.* Boston: Harvard Business School Press.

Kayser, T. A. (1990). *Mining group gold: How to cash in on the collaborative brain power of a group.* San Diego, CA: Pfeiffer & Company.

Kotter, J. P. (1996). *Leading change.* Boston: Harvard Business Review.

Larkin, T., & Larkin, S. (1996, May/June). *Reaching and changing frontline employees.* Boston: Harvard Business Review.

Larson, C. E., & LaFasto, F. M. J. (1989). *Teamwork: What must go right / What can go wrong.* Newbury Park, CA: Sage.

Lewin, K. (1953). Studies in group decision. In D. Cartwright & A. Zander (Eds.), *Group dynamics, research and theory.* Evanston, IL: Row, Peterson and Company.

Maier, N. (1963). *Problem solving discussions and conferences: Leadership methods and skills.* New York: McGraw-Hill.

Moore, C. (1986). *The mediation process. Practical strategies for resolving conflict.* San Francisco: Jossey-Bass.

Peters, T. J., & Waterman, R. H. (1982). *In search of excellence.* New York: HarperCollins.

Pfeiffer, J. W., & Jones, J. E. (1970). *Handbook of structured experiences for human relations training* (vol. II, pp. 62–67). San Diego, CA: University Associates.

Reddy, W. B. (1994). *Intervention skills: Process consultation for small groups and teams.* San Francisco: Jossey-Bass/Pfeiffer.

Ross, M. (1982). Coping with conflict. In *The 1982 annual for facilitators, trainers, and consultants.* San Diego, CA: Pfeiffer & Company.

Spector, B. (1989). From bogged down to fired up: Inspiring organizational change. *Sloan Management Review,* 29–34.

Steers, R., & Porter, L. (1983). *Motivation and work behaviour* (3rd edition). New York: McGraw-Hill.

Sundstrom, E., & Associates. (1999). *Supporting work team effectiveness.* San Francisco: Jossey-Bass.

Thomas, K. (1976). Conflict and conflict management. In M. D. Dunnette (Ed.), *Handbook of industrial and organizational psychology* (pp. 889–935). Chicago: Rand McNally College.

Von Oech, R. A. (1998). *A whack on the side of the head: How you can be more creative* (3rd edition). New York: Warner Books.

Wall, V., Jr., Galanes, G., & Love, S. (1987). Small, task-oriented groups: Conflict, conflict management, satisfaction, and decision quality. *Small Group Behavior, 18*(1), 31–55.

Weisbord, M. R. (1987). *Productive workplaces: Organizing and managing for dignity, meaning and community.* San Francisco: Jossey-Bass.

Weisbord, M. R., & Janoff, S. (1995). *Future search: An action guide to finding common ground in organizations and communities.* San Francisco: Berrett-Koehler.

Wellins, R. S., Byham, W. C., & Wilson, J. M. (1993). *Empowered teams: Creating self-directed work groups that improve quality, productivity, and participation.* San Francisco: Jossey-Bass.

Index

About the Authors

Carol A. Beatty is a leading expert in the human and organizational issues that result from implementing change and has been teaching and conducting research in this field for 18 years. She is currently Director of the Queen's University Industrial Relations Centre and Associate Professor at the Queen's School of Business. She is a sought-after speaker, consultant, and trainer for a large number of national and international clients. Dr. Beatty recently completed a major study of high-performance work teams in several Canadian organizations. Through her research, she has identified three critical sets of process skills for building high-performance teams: good team management practices, problem-solving skills, and conflict-handling skills. Dr. Beatty contributes to many journals, including *Business Quarterly*, *Sloan Management Review*, and *Human Relations*. She is author of *Employee Ownership: The New Source of Competitive Advantage* (2001).

Brenda A. Barker Scott (Master of Industrial Relations, Queen's University) is a faculty member, facilitator, and consultant at the Queen's University Industrial Relations Centre and has been helping leadership teams plan and implement systemwide change for the past 10 years. Barker Scott has rigorously field-tested the teams theory and practice with a wide variety of international clients. She designs the professional programs for the Queen's IRC certificates in Human Resources Management, Industrial Relations, and Organizational Development, and she is an adjunct professor in the School of Policy Studies. Her current research projects focus on the characteristics of teams in complex work environments.